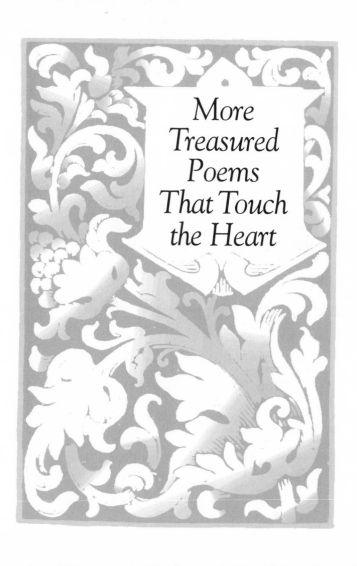

More Treasured Poems That Touch the Heart

More Treasured Poems That Touch the Heart

CHERISHED POEMS
AND FAVORITE POETS

Compiled by
MARY SANFORD LAURENCE

BRISTOL PARK BOOKS
New York

To Laura F., Amy D., and Laura C.,
the best eyes, ears, and alter egos anyone could have.

First Bristol Park Books edition published in 1997.

Bristol Park Books
A division of BBS Publishing Corporation
386 Park Avenue South
New York, NY 10016
Bristol Park Books is a registered trademark of
BBS Publishing Corporation.

Library of Congress Catalog Card Number: 97-73432
ISBN: 0-88486-171-6
Printed in the United States of America.

ACKNOWLEDGMENTS

Thanks to the following publishers for their permission to reprint the poems listed:

"Defeat" and "What's in It for Me?" reprinted from *The Collected Verse of Edgar A. Guest*, copyright © 1934; "Equipment," from *Harbor Lights of Home*, copyright © 1928; "The Kindly Neighbor," from *All That Matters* by Edgar A. Guest. Used with permission of Contemporary Books.

"The End," by Mark Van Doren from *The Collected Poems of Mark Van Doren*, © 1968 by Mark Van Doren. Reprinted by permission of Henry Holt & Co., Inc.

"Everyone Sang," copyright 1920 by E.P. Dutton, copyright renewed 1948 by Siegfried Sassoon, from *Collected Poems of Siegfried Sassoon* by Siegfried Sassoon. Used by permission of Viking Penguin, a division of Penguin Books USA Inc. Permission granted by George Sassoon to reprint this poem in Canada.

"Fleurette" from *The Collected Poems of Robert Service* by Robert Service. Copyright 1921 by Dodd Mead & Co., Inc. Used by permission of the Estate of Robert Service c/o M.W. Krasilovsky, agent, New York, NY 10017.

"Neutral Tones" reprinted with the permission of Simon & Schuster from *The Complete Poems of Thomas Hardy*, edited by James Gibson. Copyright 1925 by Macmillan Publishing Company; copyright renewed © 1953. Reprinted in Canada with

CONTENTS

In many ways, the written word conveys a sense of reality, a tangibility to emotions that we may feel totally isolated or bound by in the privacy of our own thoughts. The joyous sense of freedom, the camaraderie with another human being that we feel by emotionally connecting with thoughts on a page can be a true watershed in our lives. These are the great moments that poetry at its best can achieve with its reader.

The poems in this book were chosen for their ability to express the incredible, the ecstatic, the heartbreaking, and the profound moments that are the very pulse of life. The fragility of youth and beauty in "Ode on a Grecian Urn"; the challenge of facing the world with the strength of your own convictions posed in "If—"; the promise of perpetual kinship in the human family renewed in "I'm Nobody! Who Are You?" and the quiet hope for a safe passage home at life's journey's end expressed in "Crossing the Bar"—these elusive glimpses that have the power to reflect our own emotions and cherished memories touch us and live with us long after the book is closed. Favorite poets such as Byron, Blake, Longfellow, Wordsworth, Shakespeare, Donne, Keats, Browning, Emerson and Dickinson remain beloved because they speak to us still, generation after generation. Their words have become our connection, our own legacy of human thought, emotion and memory.

I hope this book will touch a chord in your own life.

M.S.L.

Youth

Between the dark and the daylight,
    When the night is beginning to lower,
Comes a pause in the day's occupations,
    That is known as the Children's Hour.

I hear in the chamber above me
    The patter of little feet,
The sound of a door that is opened,
    And voices soft and sweet.

From my study I see in the lamplight,
    Descending the broad hall stair,
Grave Alice, and laughing Allegra,
    And Edith with golden hair.

A whisper, and then a silence:
    Yet I know by their merry eyes
They are plotting and planning together
    To take me by surprise.

A sudden rush from the stairway,
    A sudden raid from the hall!
By three doors left unguarded
    They enter my castle wall!

They climb up into my turret
    O'er the arms and back of my chair;
If I try to escape, they surround me;
    They seem to be everywhere.

They almost devour me with kisses,
    Their arms about me entwine,
Till I think of the Bishop of Bingen
    In his Mouse-Tower on the Rhine!

Do you think, O blue-eyed banditti,
    Because you have scaled the wall,
Such an old mustache as I am
    Is not a match for you all!

I have you fast in my fortress,
    And will not let you depart,
But put you down into the dungeon
    In the round-tower of my heart.

And there will I keep you forever,
    Yes, forever and a day,
Till the walls shall crumble to ruin,
    And moulder in dust away!

HENRY WADSWORTH LONGFELLOW

Go, lovely Rose—
Tell her that wastes her time and me,
That now she knows,
When I resemble her to thee,
How sweet and fair she seems to be.

Tell her that's young,
And shuns to have her graces spied,
That hadst thou sprung
In deserts where no men abide,
Thou must have uncommended died.

Small is the worth
Of beauty from the light retired:
Bid her come forth,
Suffer herself to be desired,
And not blush so to be admired.

Then die—that she
The common fate of all things rare
May read in thee;
How small a part of time they share
That are so wondrous sweet and fair!

EDMUND WALLER

Beware fair maid of musky courtiers' oaths,
Take heed what gifts and favors you receive,
Let not the fading gloss of silken clothes
Dazzle your virtue, or your fame bereave.
    For lose but once the hold you have of grace,
    Who'll e'er respect your fortune or your face?

Each greedy hand will strive to catch the flower
When none regards the stalk it grows upon,
Each creature seeks the fruit still to devour
But leave the tree to fall or stand alone.
    Yet this advice, fair creature, take of me,
    Let none take fruit, unless he take the tree.

Believe no oaths, nor much protesting men,
Credit no vows, nor no bewailing songs,
Let courtiers swear, forswear, and swear again;
Their hearts do live ten regions from their tongues.
    For when with oaths they make thy heart to tremble
    Believe them least, for then they most dissemble.

Beware lest Caesar do corrupt thy mind
Or fond Ambition sell thy modesty.
Say though a king thou ever courteous find
He cannot garden thy virginity.
    Begin with king, to subject you will fall,
    From lord to lackey, and at last to all.

AUTHOR UNKNOWN

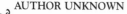

I have a garden of my own,
    Shining with flowers of every hue;
I loved it dearly while alone,
    But I shall love it more with you:
And there the golden bees shall come,
    In summer time at break of morn,
And wake us with their busy hum
    Around the Siha's fragrant thorn.
I have a fawn from Aden's land,
    On leafy buds and berries nursed;
And you shall feed him from your hand,
    Though he may start with fear at first,
And I will lead you where he lies
    For shelter in the noon-tide heat;
And you may touch his sleeping eyes,
    And feel his little silvery feet.

THOMAS MOORE

INFANT JOY

"I have no name:
"I am but two days old."
What shall I call thee?
"I happy am,
"Joy is my name."
Sweet joy befall thee!

Pretty joy!
Sweet joy but two days old,
Sweet joy I call thee:
Thou dost smile,
I sing the while,
Sweet joy befall thee!

WILLIAM BLAKE

HOW OLD ARE YOU?

Age is a quality of mind.
If you have left your dreams behind,
If hope is cold,
If you no longer look ahead,
If your ambitions' fires are dead—
Then you are old.

But if from life you take the best,
And if in life you keep the jest,
If love you hold;
No matter how the years go by,
No matter how the birthdays fly—
You are not old.

H.S. FRITSCH

Life

I am a parcel of vain strivings tied
　　By a chance bond together,
　Dangling this way and that, their links
　　Were made so loose and wide,
　　　Methinks,
　　For milder weather.

A bunch of violets without their roots,
　　And sorrel intermixed,
　Encircled by a wisp of straw
　　Once coiled about their shoots,
　　　The law
　　By which I'm fixed.

A nosegay which Time clutched from out
　　Those fair Elysian fields,
　With weeds and broken stems, in haste,
　　Doth make the rabble rout
　　　That waste
　　The day he yields.

And here I bloom for a short hour unseen,
　　Drinking my juices up,
　With no root in the land
　　To keep my branches green,
　　　But stand
　　In a bare cup.

Some tender buds were left upon my stem
    In mimicry of life,
  But ah! the children will not know,
    Till time has withered them,
      The woe
    With which they're rife.

But now I see I was not plucked for naught,
    And after in life's vase
  Of glass set while I might survive,
    But by a kind hand brought
      Alive
    To a strange place.

That stock thus thinned will soon redeem its hours,
    And by another year,
  Such as God knows, with freer air,
    More fruits and fairer flowers
      Will bear,
    While I droop here.

HENRY DAVID THOREAU

There is sweet music here that softer falls
Than petals from blown roses on the grass,
Or night-dews on still waters between walls
Of shadowy granite, in a gleaming pass;
Music that gentlier on the spirit lies,
Than tired eyelids upon tired eyes;
Music that brings sweet sleep down from the blissful
    skies.
Here are cool mosses deep,
And thro' the moss the ivies creep,
And in the stream the long-leaved flowers weep,
And from the craggy ledge the poppy hangs in sleep.

Why are we weigh'd upon with heaviness,
And utterly consumed with sharp distress,
While all things else have rest from weariness?
All things have rest: why should we toil alone,
We only toil, who are the first of things,
And make perpetual moan,
Still from one sorrow to another thrown:
Nor ever fold our wings,
And cease from wanderings,
Nor steep our brows in slumber's holy balm;
Nor harken what the inner spirit sings,
'There is no joy but calm!' —
Why should we only toil, the roof and crown of
    things?

Lo! in the middle of the wood,
The folded leaf is woo'd from out the bud
With winds upon the branch, and there
Grows green and broad, and takes no care,
Sun-steep'd at noon, and in the moon
Nightly dew-fed; and turning yellow
Falls, and floats adown the air.
Lo! sweeten'd with the summer light,
The full-juiced apple, waxing over-mellow,
Drops in a silent autumn night.
All its allotted length of days,
The flower ripens in its place,
Ripens and fades, and falls, and hath no toil,
Fast-rooted in the fruitful soil.

Hateful is the dark-blue sky,
Vaulted o'er the dark-blue sea.
Death is the end of life; ah, why
Should life all labour be?
Let us alone. Time driveth onward fast,
And in a little while our lips are dumb.
Let us alone. What is it that will last?
All things are taken from us, and become
Portions and parcels of the dreadful Past.
Let us alone. What pleasure can we have
To war with evil? Is there any peace
In ever climbing up the climbing wave?

All things have rest, and ripen toward the grave
In silence; ripen, fall and cease:
Give us long rest or death, dark death, or dreamful ease.

How sweet it were, hearing the downward stream,
With half-shut eyes ever to seem
Falling asleep in a half-dream!
To dream and dream, like yonder amber light,
Which will not leave the myrrh-bush on the height;
To hear each other's whisper'd speech;
Eating the Lotus day by day,
To watch the crisping ripples on the beach,
And tender curving lines of creamy spray;
To lend our hearts and spirits wholly
To the influence of mild-minded melancholy;
To muse and brood and live again in memory,
With those old faces of our infancy
Heap'd over with a mound of grass,
Two handfuls of white dust, shut in an urn of brass!

Dear is the memory of our wedded lives,
And dear the last embraces of our wives
And their warm tears: but all hath suffer'd change:
For surely now our household hearths are cold:
Our sons inherit us: our looks are strange:
And we should come like ghosts to trouble joy.

Or else the island princes over-bold
Have eat our substance, and the minstrel sings
Before them of the ten years' war in Troy,
And our great deeds, as half-forgotten things.
Is there confusion in the little isle?
Let what is broken so remain.
The Gods are hard to reconcile:
'Tis hard to settle order once again.
There *is* confusion worse than death,
Trouble on trouble, pain on pain,
Long labour unto aged breath,
Sore task to hearts worn out with many wars
And eyes grown dim with gazing on the pilot-stars.

But propt on beds of amaranth and moly,
How sweet (while warm airs lull us, blowing lowly)
With half-dropt eyelids still,
Beneath a heaven dark and holy,
To watch the long bright river drawing slowly
His waters from the purple hill—
To hear the dewy echoes calling
From cave to cave thro' the thick-twinèd vine—
To watch the emerald-colour'd water falling
Thro' many a wov'n acanthus-wreath divine!
Only to hear and see the far-off sparkling brine,
Only to hear were sweet, stretch'd out beneath the pine.

The Lotos blooms below the barren peak:
The Lotos blows by every winding creek:
All day the wind breathes low with mellower tone:
Thro' every hollow cave and alley lone
Round and round the spicy downs the yellow Lotos-
dust is blown.
We have had enough of action, and of motion we,
Roll'd to starboard, roll'd to larboard, when the surge
was seething free,
Where the wallowing monster spouted his foam-foun-
tains in the sea.
Let us swear an oath, and keep it with an equal mind,
In the hollow Lotos-land to live and lie reclined
On the hills like Gods together, careless of mankind.
For they lie beside their nectar, and the bolts are
hurl'd
Far below them in the valleys, and the clouds are
lightly curl'd
Round their golden houses, girdled with the gleaming
world:
Where they smile in secret, looking over wasted lands,
Blight and famine, plague and earthquake, roaring
deeps and fiery sands,
Clanging fights, and flaming towns, and sinking ships,
and praying hands.
But they smile, they find a music centred in a doleful
song

Steaming up, a lamentation and an ancient tale of
   wrong,
Like a tale of little meaning tho' the words are strong;
Chanted from an ill-used race of men that cleave the
   soil,
Sow the seed, and reap the harvest with enduring toil,
Storing yearly little dues of wheat, and wine and oil;
Till they perish and they suffer—some, 'tis whisper'd—
   down in hell
Suffer endless anguish, others in Elysian valleys dwell,
Resting weary limbs at last on beds of asphodel.
Surely, surely, slumber is more sweet than toil, the
   shore
Than labour in the deep mid-ocean, wind and wave
   and oar;
O rest ye, brother mariners, we will not wander more.

ALFRED, LORD TENNYSON

Think thou and act; to-morrow thou shalt die.
    Outstretch'd in the sun's warmth upon the shore,
    Thou say'st: 'Man's measured path is all gone o'er:
Up all his years, steeply, with strain and sigh,
Man clomb until he touch'd the truth; and I,
    Even I, am he whom it was destined for.'
    How should this be? Art thou then so much more
Than they who sow'd, that thou shouldst reap thereby?

Nay, come up hither. From this wave-wash'd mound
    Unto the furthest flood-brim look with me;
Then reach on with thy thought till it be drown'd.
    Miles and miles distant though the last line be,
And though thy soul sail leagues and leagues beyond,—
    Still, leagues beyond those leagues, there is more sea.

DANTE GABRIEL ROSSETTI

LAMENT

Adieu, farewell earths blisse,
This world uncertaine is,
Fond are lifes lustfull joyes,
Death proves them all but toyes,
None from his darts can flye,
I am sick, I must dye:
　　Lord have mercy on us.

Rich men, trust not in wealth,
Gold cannot buy you health,
Phisick himselfe must fade.
All things, to end are made,
The plague full swift goes bye,
I am sick, I must dye:
　　Lord have mercy on us.

Beauty is but a flowre,
Which wrinckles will devoure,
Brightness falls from the ayre,
Queenes have died yong, and faire,
Dust hath closde *Helens* eye.
I am sick, I must dye:
　　Lord have mercy on us.

Strength stoopes unto the grave,
Wormes feed on *Hector* brave,
Swords may not fight with fate,

Earth still holds ope her gate.
Come, come, the bells do crye.
I am sick, I must dye:
    Lord have mercy on us.

Wit with his wantonesse,
Tasteth deaths bitterness:
Hels executioner,
Hath no eares for to heare
What vaine art can reply.
I am sick, I must dye:
    Lord have mercy on us.

Haste therefore eche degree,
To welcome destiny:
Heaven is our heritage,
Earth but a players stage,
Mount wee unto the sky.
I am sick, I must dye:
    Lord have mercy on us.

THOMAS NASHE

MY MIND TO ME A KINGDOM IS

My mind to me a kingdom is,
 Such present joys therein I find,
That it excels all other bliss
 That earth affords or grows by kind:
Though much I want which most would have,
Yet still my mind forbids to crave.

No princely pomp, no wealthy store,
 No force to win the victory,
No wily wit to salve a sore,
 No shape to feed a loving eye;
To none of these I yield as thrall:
For why? My mind doth serve for all.

I see how plenty [surfeits] oft,
 And hasty climbers soon do fall;
I see that those which are aloft
 Mishap doth threaten most of all;
They get with toil, they keep with fear:
Such cares my mind could never bear.

Content to live, this is my stay;
 I seek no more than may suffice;
I press to bear no haughty sway;
 Look, what I lack my mind supplies:
Lo, thus I triumph like a king,
Content with that my mind doth bring.

Some have too much, yet still do crave;
   I little have, and seek no more.
They are but poor, though much they have,
   And I am rich with little store;
They poor, I rich; they beg, I give;
They lack, I leave; they pine, I live.

I laugh not at another's loss;
   I grudge not at another's gain;
No worldly waves my mind can toss;
   My state at one doth still remain:
I fear no foe, I fawn no friend;
I loathe not life, nor dread my end.

Some weigh their pleasure by their lust,
   Their wisdom by their rage of will;
Their treasure is their only trust;
   A cloakèd craft their store of skill:
But all the pleasure that I find
Is to maintain a quiet mind.

My wealth is health and perfect ease;
   My conscience clear my chief defense;
I neither seek by bribes to please,
   Nor by deceit to breed offense:
Thus do I live; thus will I die;
Would all did so as well as I!

SIR EDWARD DYER

Art thou poor, yet hast thou golden slumbers?
   O sweet content!
Art thou rich, yet is thy mind perplex'd?
   O punishment!
Dost thou laugh to see how fools are vex'd
To add to golden numbers golden numbers?
   O sweet content! O sweet, O sweet content!
Work apace, apace, apace, apace;
Honest labour bears a lovely face;
Then hey nonny nonny—hey nonny nonny!

Canst drink the waters of the crispèd spring?
   O sweet content!
Swim'st thou in wealth, yet sink'st in thine own tears?
   O punishment!
Then he that patiently want's burden bears,
No burden bears, but is a king, a king!
   O sweet content! O sweet, O sweet content!
Work apace, apace, apace, apace;
Honest labour bears a lovely face;
Then hey nonny nonny—hey nonny nonny!

THOMAS DEKKER

BE KIND

Be kind to thy father: for when thou wert young,
    Who loved thee as fondly as he?
He caught the first accents that fell from thy tongue,
    And joined in thine innocent glee.

Be kind to thy mother: for lo! on her brow
    May traces of sorrow be seen;
Oh, well may'st thou cherish and comfort her now
    For loving and kind hath she been.

Be kind to thy brother: wherever you are,
    The love of a brother shall be
An ornament, purer and richer by far
    Than pearls from the depths of the sea.

Be kind to thy sister: not many may know
    The depth of true sisterly love;
The wealth of the ocean lies fathoms below
    The surface that sparkles above.

Thy kindness shall bring to thee many sweet hours,
    And blessings thy pathway to crown;
Affection shall weave thee a garland of flowers,
    More precious than wealth or renown.

MARGARET COURTNEY

YOU NEVER CAN TELL

You never can tell when you send a word
    Like an arrow shot from a bow
By an archer blind, be it cruel or kind,
    Just where it may chance to go.
It may pierce the breast of your dearest friend,
    Tipped with its poison or balm,
To a stranger's heart in life's great mart
    It may carry its pain or its calm.

You never can tell when you do an act
    Just what the result will be,
But with every deed you are sowing a seed,
    Though the harvest you may not see.
Each kindly act is an acorn dropped
    In God's productive soil;
You may not know, but the tree shall grow
    With shelter for those who toil.

You never can tell what your thoughts will do
    In bringing you hate or love,
For thoughts are things, and their airy wings
    Are swifter than carrier doves.
They follow the law of the universe—
    Each thing must create its kind,
And they speed o'er the track to bring you back
    Whatever went out from your mind.

ELLA WHEELER WILCOX

I saw two clouds at morning,
    Tinged with the rising sun,
And in the dawn they floated on,
    And mingled into one:
I thought that morning cloud was blest,
It moved so sweetly to the west.

I saw two summer currents
    Flow smoothly to their meeting,
And join their course, with silent force,
    In peace each other greeting:
Calm was their course through banks of green,
While dimpling eddies played between.

Such be your gentle motion,
    Till life's last pulse shall beat;
Like summer's beam, and summer's stream,
    Float on, in joy, to meet
A calmer sea, where storms shall cease—
A purer sky, where all is peace.

JOHN GARDINER BRAINARD

THE CLOWN

A crowd was gathering beneath the tent—
   The clown must keep them in a happy mood;
   No matter if the jokes are rough and rude,
A circus is a place for merriment.
And one must be quick-minded and invent
   New tricks and let no saddened thoughts intrude,
   Nor let the public see him sigh or brood,
But banish care and seem indifferent.

There came a lull—I saw him lean awhile
   Against a post and gaze with weary eyes,
As if he traveled backward many a mile. . . .
   And though his body wore a gay disguise,
For one brief space he played a tragic role—
There is no mask to hide a lonely soul.

MARGARET E. BRUNER

IF YOU MADE GENTLER THE CHURLISH WORLD

If you have spoken something beautiful,
Or touched the dead canvas to life,
Or made the cold stone to speak—
You who know the secret heart of beauty;
If you have done one thing
That has made gentler the churlish world,
Though mankind pass you by,
And feed and clothe you grudgingly—
Though the world starve you,
And God answer not your nightly prayers,
And you grow old hungering still at heart,
And walk friendless in your way,
And lie down at last forgotten—
If all this befall you who have created beauty,
You shall still leave a bequest to the world
Greater than institutions and riches and commerce;
And by the immutable law of the human heart
The God of the universe is your debtor,
If you have made gentler the churlish world.

MAX EHRMANN

ROOF-TOPS

Roof-tops, roof-tops, what do you cover?
Sad folk, bad folk, and many a glowing lover;
Wise people, simple people, children of despair—
Roof-tops, roof-tops, hiding pain and care.

Roof-tops, roof-tops, O what sin you're knowing,
While above you in the sky the white clouds are
   blowing.
While beneath you, agony and dolor and grim strife
Fight the olden battle, the olden war of Life.

Roof-tops, roof-tops, cover up their shame—
Wretched souls, prisoned souls too piteous to name;
Man himself hath built you all to hide away the
   stars—
Roof-tops, roof-tops, you hide ten million scars.

Roof-tops, roof-tops, well I know you cover
Many solemn tragedies, and many a lonely lover;
But, ah! you hide the good that lives in the throbbing
   city—
Patient wives, and tenderness, forgiveness, faith, and
   pity. . . .

CHARLES HANSON TOWNE

The common tasks are beautiful if we
Have eyes to see their shining ministry.
The plowman with his share deep in the loam;
The carpenter whose skilled hands build a home;
The gardener working with reluctant sod,
Faithful to his partnership with God—
These are the artisans of life. And, oh,
A woman with her eyes and cheeks aglow,
Watching a kettle, tending a scarlet flame,
Guarding a little child—there is no name
For these great ministries, and eyes are dull
That do not see that they are beautiful;
That do not see within the common tasks
The simple answer to the thing God asks
Of any child, a pride within His breast;
That at our given work we do our best.

GRACE NOLL CROWELL

We fancied he'd share in our cause. Instead,
"There is nothing in it for me!" he said.
He passed up pity and play and mirth
And counted his time to the penny's worth.
Ask for his help, and this would be
His answer: "What is there in it for me?"

Nothing it meant if you said: "In this
Perhaps is friendship you'll some day miss.
Here is a task that won't pay in gold,
But will leave you prouder when you grow old.
Though nothing for this will your purse collect,
It will pay you richly in self-respect."

"What is there in it for me?" he said.
We mentioned pride, but he shook his head.
"The joy of giving," he flicked his hand—
That he never could understand.
And he found when life's last far bend was turned
That money was all he had ever earned.

EDGAR A. GUEST

HOLIDAYS

The holiest of all holidays are those
Kept by ourselves in silence and apart;
The secret anniversaries of the heart.

HENRY WADSWORTH LONGFELLOW

THE VILLAGE BLACKSMITH

Under a spreading chestnut tree
    The village smithy stands;
The smith, a mighty man is he,
    With large and sinewy hands;
And the muscles of his brawny arms
    Are strong as iron bands.

His hair is crisp, and black, and long,
    His face is like the tan;
His brow is wet with honest sweat,
    He earns whate'er he can,
And looks the whole world in the face,
    For he owes not any man.
Week in, week out, from morn till night,
    You can hear his bellows blow;
You can hear him swing his heavy sledge,
    With measured beat and slow,
Like a sexton ringing the village bell,
    When the evening sun is low.

And children coming home from school
    Look in at the open door;
They love to see the flaming forge,
    And hear the bellows roar,
And catch the burning sparks that fly
    Like chaff from a threshing floor.

He goes on Sunday to the church,
    And sits among his boys;
He hears the parson pray and preach,
    He hears his daughter's voice,
Singing in the village choir,
    And it makes his heart rejoice.

It sounds to him like her mother's voice,
    Singing in Paradise!
He needs must think of her once more,
    How in the grave she lies;
And with his hard, rough hand he wipes
    A tear out of his eyes.

Toiling,—rejoicing,—sorrowing,
    Onward through life he goes;
Each morning sees some task begin,
    Each evening sees it close;
Something attempted, something done,
    Has earned a night's repose.
Thanks, thanks to thee, my worthy friend,
    For the lesson thou hast taught!
Thus at the flaming forge of life
    Our fortunes must be wrought;
Thus on its sounding anvil shaped
    Each burning deed and thought!

HENRY WADSWORTH LONGFELLOW

IF I CAN STOP ONE HEART FROM BREAKING

If I can stop one heart from breaking,
   I shall not live in vain;
If I can ease one life the aching,
   Or cool one pain,
Or help one lonely person
   Into happiness again
I shall not live in vain.

EMILY DICKINSON

There! little girl; don't cry!
   They have broken your doll, I know;
      And your tea-set blue,
      And your play-house, too,
   Are things of the long ago;
      But childish troubles will soon pass by
      There! little girl; don't cry!

There! little girl; don't cry!
   They have broken your slate, I know;
      And the glad, wild ways
      of your school-girl days
   Are things of the long ago;
      But life and love will soon come by.
      There! little girl; don't cry!

There! little girl; don't cry!
   They have broken your heart, I know;
      And the rainbow gleams
      Of your youthful dreams
   Are things of the long ago;
      But heaven holds all for which you sigh.
      There! little girl; don't cry!

JAMES WHITCOMB RILEY

IF—

If you can keep your head when all about you
    Are losing theirs and blaming it on you;
If you can trust yourself when all men doubt you,
    But make allowance for their doubting too;
If you can wait and not be tired by waiting,
    Or, being lied about, don't deal in lies,
Or, being hated, don't give way to hating,
    And yet don't look too good, nor talk too wise;

If you can dream—and not make dreams your master;
If you can think—and not make thoughts your aim;
If you can meet with triumph and disaster
    And treat those two impostors just the same;
If you can bear to hear the truth you've spoken
    Twisted by knaves to make a trap for fools,
Or watch the things you gave your life to broken,
    And stoop and build 'em up with worn out tools;

If you can make one heap of all your winnings
    And risk it on one turn of pitch-and-toss,
And lose, and start again at your beginnings
    And never breathe a word about your loss;
If you can force your heart and nerve and sinew
    To serve your turn long after they are gone,
And so hold on when there is nothing in you
    Except the Will which says to them: "Hold on!"

If you can talk with crowds and keep your virtue,
 Or walk with kings—nor lose the common touch;
If neither foes nor loving friends can hurt you;
 If all men count with you, but none too much;
If you can fill the unforgiving minute
 With sixty seconds' worth of distance run—
Yours is the Earth and everything that's in it,
 And—which is more—you'll be a Man, my son!

RUDYARD KIPLING

COMMONPLACE

"A commonplace life," we say, and we sigh,
But why should we sigh as we say?
The commonplace sun in the commonplace sky
Makes up the commonplace day;
The moon and the stars are commonplace things,
And the flower that blooms, and the bird that sings,
But dark were the world, and sad our lot,
If the flowers failed, and the sun shone not;
And God, who studies each separate soul,
Out of commonplace lives makes His beautiful whole.

SUSAN COOLIDGE

Hark, how the birds do sing,
    And woods do ring!
All creatures have their joy, and man hath his.
    Yet if we rightly measure,
    Man's joy and pleasure
Rather hereafter than in present is.

    To this life things of sense
        Make their pretence;
In th' other angels have a right by birth.
    Man ties them both alone,
    And makes them one,
With th' one hand touching Heav'n, with th' other
    earth.

    In soul he mounts and flies,
        In flesh he dies.
He wears a stuff whose thread is coarse and round,
    But trimmed with curious lace,
    And should take place
After the trimming, not the stuff and ground.

    Not that he may not here
        Taste of the cheer;
But as birds drink and straight lift up their head,
    So must he sip and think

Of better drink
He may attain to after he is dead.

But as his joys are double,
    So is his trouble.
He hath two winters, other things but one.
    Both frosts and thoughts do nip
    And bite his lip,
And he of all things fears two deaths alone.

Yet ev'n the greatest griefs
    May be reliefs,
Could he but take them right and in their ways.
    Happy is he whose heart
    Hath found the art
To turn his double pains to double praise.

GEORGE HERBERT

THE WISH

Well then, I now do plainly see
This busy world and I shall ne'er agree;
The very honey of all earthly joy
    Does of all meats the soonest cloy,
    And they methinks deserve my pity
Who for it can endure the stings,
The crowd and buzz and murmurings
    Of this great hive, the city.

Ah, yet, ere I descend to th' grave
May I a small house and large garden have!
And a few friends and many books, both true,
    Both wise and both delightful too!
    And since love ne'er will from me flee,
A mistress moderately fair,
And good as guardian-angels are,
    Only beloved and loving me!

O fountains, when in you shall I
Myself eased of unpeaceful thoughts espy?
O fields, O woods, when, when shall I be made
    The happy tenant of your shade?
    Here's the spring-head of pleasure's flood;
Here's wealthy Nature's treasury,
Where all the riches lie that she
    Has coined and stamped for good.

Pride and ambition here
Only in far-fetched metaphors appear;
Here nought but winds can hurtful murmurs scatter,
    And nought but echo flatter.
    The gods when they descended hither
From heaven did always choose their way;
And therefore we may boldly say,
    That 'tis the way too thither.

    How happy here should I
And one dear she live and embracing die!
She who is all the world, and can exclude
    In deserts solitude.
    I should have then this only fear,
Lest men, when they my pleasures see,
Should hither throng to live like me,
    And so make a city here.

ABRAHAM COWLEY

Love

When our two souls stand up erect and strong,
   Face to face, silent, drawing nigh and nigher,
   Until the lengthening wings break into fire
At either curving point,—what bitter wrong
Can the earth do us, that we should not long
   Be here contented? Think! In mounting higher,
   The angels would press on us, and aspire
To drop some golden orb of perfect song
Into our deep, dear silence. Let us stay
   Rather on earth, Belovèd—where the unfit
Contrarious moods of men recoil away
   And isolate pure spirits, and permit
A place to stand and love in for a day,
   With darkness and the death-hour rounding it.

ELIZABETH BARRETT BROWNING

A MATCH

If love were what the rose is,
    And I were like the leaf,
Our lives would grow together
In sad or singing weather,
Blown fields or flowerful closes,
    Green pleasure or gray grief;
If love were what the rose is,
    And I were like the leaf.

If I were what the words are,
    And love were like the tune,
With double sound and single
Delight our lips would mingle,
With kisses glad as birds are
    That get sweet rain at noon;
If I were what the words are,
    And love were like the tune.

If you were life, my darling,
    And I, your love, were death,
We'd shine and snow together
Ere March made sweet the weather
With daffodil and starling
    And hours of fruitful breath;
If you were life, my darling,
    And I, your love, were death.

If you were thrall to sorrow,
    And I were page to joy,
We'd play for lives and seasons,
With loving looks and treasons,
And tears of night and morrow,
    And laughs of maid and boy;
If you were thrall to sorrow,
    And I were page to joy.

If you were April's lady,
    And I were lord in May,
We'd throw with leaves for hours,
And draw for days with flowers,
Till day like night were shady,
    And night were bright like day;
If you were April's lady,
    And I were lord in May.

If you were queen of pleasure,
    And I were king of pain,
We'd hunt down love together,
Pluck out his flying-feather,
And teach his feet a measure,
    And find his mouth a rein;
If you were queen of pleasure,
    And I were king of pain.

ALGERNON CHARLES SWINBURNE

MEMORY

My mind lets go a thousand things,
Like dates of wars and deaths of kings,
And yet recalls the very hour—
'Twas noon by yonder village tower,
And on the last blue noon in May—
The wind came briskly up this way,
Crisping the brook beside the road;
Then, pausing here, set down its load
Of pine-scents, and shook listlessly
Two petals from that wild-rose tree.

THOMAS BAILEY ALDRICH

IT IS NOT BEAUTY I DEMAND

It is not Beauty I demand,
   A crystal brow, the moon's despair,
Nor the snow's daughter, a white hand,
   Nor mermaid's yellow pride of hair.

Tell me not of your starry eyes,
   Your lips that seem on roses fed,
Your breasts where Cupid trembling lies,
   Nor sleeps for kissing of his bed.

A bloomy pair of vermeil cheeks,
   Like Hebe's in her ruddiest hours,
A breath that softer music speaks
   Than summer winds a-wooing flowers.

These are but gauds; nay, what are lips?
   Coral beneath the ocean-stream,
Whose brink when your adventurer sips
   Full oft he perisheth on them.

And what are cheeks but ensigns oft
   That wave hot youth to fields of blood?
Did Helen's breast though ne'er so soft,
   Do Greece or Ilium any good?

Eyes can with baleful ardor burn,
    Poison can breath that erst perfumed,
There's many a white hand holds an urn
    With lovers' hearts to dust consumed.

For crystal brows—there's naught within,
    They are but empty cells for pride;
He who the Syren's hair would win
    Is mostly strangled in the tide.

Give me, instead of beauty's bust,
    A tender heart, a loyal mind,
Which with temptation I could trust,
    Yet never linked with error find.

One in whose gentle bosom I
    Could pour my secret heart of woes,
Like the care-burdened honey-fly
    That hides his murmurs in the rose.

My earthly comforter! whose love
    So indefeasible might be,
That when my spirit won above
    Hers could not stay for sympathy.

GEORGE DARLEY

Go fetch to me a pint o' wine,
    An' fill it in a silver tassie,
That I may drink, before I go,
    A service to my bonnie lassie.
The boat rocks at the pier o' Leith,
    Fu' loud the wind blaws frae the ferry,
The ship rides by the Berwick-law,
    And I maun leave my bonnie Mary.

The trumpets sound, the banners fly,
    The glittering spears are rankèd ready;
The shouts o' war are heard afar,
    The battle closes thick and bloody;
But it's no the roar o' sea or shore
    Wad mak me langer wish to tarry;
Nor shout o' war that's heard afar—
    It's leaving thee, my bonnie Mary!

ROBERT BURNS

TO ALTHEA, FROM PRISON

When Love with unconfinèd wings
    Hovers within my gates,
And my divine Althea brings
    To whisper at the grates;
When I lie tangled in her hair
    And fetter'd to her eye,
The birds that wanton in the air
    Know no such liberty.

When flowing cups run swiftly round
    With no allaying Thames,
Our careless heads with roses bound,
    Our hearts with loyal flames;
When thirsty grief in wine we steep,
    When healths and draughts go free—
Fishes that tipple in the deep
    Know no such liberty.

When, like committed linnets, I
    With shriller throat shall sing
The sweetness, mercy, majesty,
    And glories of my King;
When I shall voice aloud how good
    He is, how great should be,
Enlargèd winds, that curl the flood,
    Know no such liberty.

Stone walls do not a prison make,
    Nor iron bars a cage;
Minds innocent and quiet take
    That for an hermitage;
If I have freedom in my love
    And in my soul am free,
Angels alone, that soar above,
    Enjoy such liberty.

RICHARD LOVELACE

When I consider how my light is spent,
   E're half my days, in this dark world and wide,
   And that one Talent which is death to hide,
   Lodg'd with me useless, though my Soul more bent
To serve therewith my Maker, and present
   My true account, least he returning chide,
   Doth God exact day-labour, light deny'd,
   I fondly ask; But patience to prevent
That murmur, soon replies, God doth not need
   Either man's work or his own gifts, who best
   Bear his milde yoak, they serve him best, his State
Is Kingly. Thousands at his bidding speed
   And post o're Land and Ocean without rest:
They also serve who only stand and waite.

JOHN MILTON

UNHAPPY VERSE

Unhappy Verse, the witnesse of my unhappie state,
  Make thy selfe fluttring wings of thy fast flying
  Thought, and fly forth unto my Love, whersoever she
  be:
Whether lying reastlesse in heavy bed, or else
  Sitting so cheerelesse at the cheerfull boord, or else
  Playing alone carelesse on her heavenlie Virginals.
If in Bed, tell her that my eyes can take no rest;
  If at Boord, tell her that my mouth can eat no meate;
  If at her Virginals, tell her I can heare no mirth.
Asked why? say, Waking Love suffereth no sleepe;
  Say that raging Love doth appall the weak stomacke;
  Say that lamenting Love marreth the Musicall.
Tell her that her pleasures were wonte to lull me asleepe;
  Tell her that her beautie was wonte to feede mine eyes;
  Tell her that her sweete Tongue was wont to make me
    mirth.
Nowe do I nightly waste, wanting my kindely rest;
  Nowe do I dayly starve, wanting my lively food?
  Nowe do I alwayes dye, wanting thy timely mirth.
And if I waste, who will bewaile my heavy chaunce?
  And if I starve, who will record my cursed end?
  And if I dye, who will saye, *this was Immerito?*

EDMUND SPENSER

WHY DO I LOVE YOU?

I love you,
Not only for what you are,
But for what I am
When I am with you.

I love you
Not only for what
You have made of yourself,
But for what
You are making of me.

I love you
For ignoring the possibilities
Of the fool in me
And for laying firm hold
Of the possibilities for good.

Why do I love you?

I love you
For closing your eyes
To the discords—
And for adding to the music in me
By worshipful listening.

I love you because you
Are helping me to make
Of the lumber of my life
Not a tavern
But a temple;
And out of the words
Of my every day
Not a reproach
But a song.

I love you
Because you have done
More than any creed
To make me happy.

You have done it
Without a word,
Without a touch,
Without a sign.
You have done it
Just by being yourself.

After all
Perhaps that is what
Love means.

ROY CROFT

TELL HER SO

Amid the cares of married strife
   In spite of toil and business life
If you value your dear wife—
   Tell her so!

When days are dark and deeply blue
   She has her troubles, same as you
Show her that your love is true
   Tell her so!

Don't act as if she's past her prime
   As tho' to please her were a crime
If ever you loved her, now's the time—
   Tell her so!

She'll return for each caress
   A hundred fold of tenderness,
Hearts like hers were made to bless;
   Tell her so!

You are hers and hers alone;
   Well you know she's all your own;
Don't wait to carve it on a stone—
   Tell her so!

Never let her heart grow cold
   Richer beauties will unfold
She is worth her weight in gold
   Tell her so!

AUTHOR UNKNOWN

FULFILLMENT

Lo, I have opened unto you the
    gates of my being,
And like a tide, you have flowed
    into me.
The innermost recesses of my spirit
    are full of you
And all the channels of my soul
    are grown sweet with your presence
For you have brought me peace;
    The peace of great tranquil waters,
And the quiet of the summer sea.
    Your hands are filled with peace as
The noon-tide is filled with light;
    About your head is bound the eternal
Quiet of the stars, and in your heart
    dwells the calm miracle of twilight.

I am utterly content.

In all my being is no ripple of unrest
    For I have opened unto you the
Wide gates of my being
    And like a tide, you have flowed into me.

AUTHOR UNKNOWN

AT A WINDOW

Give me hunger,
O you gods that sit and give
The world its orders.
Give me hunger, pain and want;
Shut me out with shame and failure
From your doors of gold and fame,
Give me your shabbiest, weariest hunger.
But leave me a little love;
A voice to speak to me in the day-end,
A hand to touch me in the dark room,
Breaking the long loneliness.
In the dusk of day-shapes,
Blurring the sunset,
One little wandering, western star
Thrust out from the changing shores of shadow.
Let me go to the window,
Watch there the day-shapes of dusk,
And wait and know the coming
Of a little love.

CARL SANDBURG

FOR LOVE'S SAKE ONLY

If thou must love me, let it be for nought
Except for love's sake only. Do not say
"I love her for her smile—her look—her way
Of speaking gently,—for a trick of thought
That falls in well with mine, and certes brought
A sense of pleasant ease on such a day"—
For these things in themselves, Beloved, may
Be changed, or change for thee,—and love, so wrought,
May be unwrought so. Neither love me for
Thine own dear pity's wiping my cheeks dry,—
A creature might forget to weep, who bore
Thy comfort long, and lose thy love thereby!
But love me for love's sake, that evermore
Thou mayst love on, through love's eternity.

ELIZABETH BARRETT BROWNING

NIGHTFALL

I need so much the quiet of your love
After the day's loud strife;
I need your calm all other things above
After the stress of life.

I crave the haven that in your dear heart lies,
After all toil is done,
I need the star shine of your heavenly eyes,
After the day's great sun.

CHARLES HANSON TOWNE

I

Thou still unravish'd bride of quietness.
 Thou foster-child of silence and slow time,
Sylvan historian, who canst thus express
 A flowery tale more sweetly than our rhyme:
What leaf-fring'd legend haunts about the shape
 Of deities or mortals, or of both,
  In Tempe or the dales of Arcady?
 What men or gods are these? What maidens loth?
What mad pursuit? What struggle to escape?
 What pipes and timbrels? What wild ecstasy?

II

Heard melodies are sweet, but those unheard
 Are sweeter; therefore, ye soft pipes, play on;
Not to the sensual ear, but, more endear'd,
 Pipe to the spirit ditties of no tone:
Fair youth, beneath the trees, thou canst not leave
 Thy song, nor ever can those trees be bare;
  Bold Lover, never, never canst thou kiss,
Though winning near the goal—yet, do not grieve;
 She cannot fade, though thou hast not thy bliss,
  For ever wilt thou love, and she be fair!
Ah, happy, happy boughs! that cannot shed

Your leaves, nor ever bid the Spring adieu;
And, happy melodist, unwearied,
    Forever piping songs forever new;
More happy love! more happy, happy love!
    Forever warm and still to be enjoy'd,
        Forever panting, and forever young;
All breathing human passion far above,
    That leaves a heart high-sorrowful and cloy'd,
        A burning forehead, and a parching tongue.

III

Who are these coming to the sacrifice?
    To what green altar, O mysterious priest,
Lead'st thou that heifer lowing at the skies,
    And all her silken flanks with garlands drest?
What little town by river or sea shore,
    Or mountain-built with peaceful citadel,
        Is emptied of this folk, this pious morn
And, little town, thy streets for evermore
    Will silent be; and not a soul to tell
        Why thou art desolate, can e'er return.

IV

O Attic shape! Fair attitude! with brede
    Of marble men and maidens overwrought,

With forest branches and the trodden weed;
    Thou, silent form, dost tease us out of thought
As doth eternity: Cold Pastoral!
  When old age shall this generation waste,
    Thou shalt remain, in midst of other woe
Than ours, a friend to man, to whom thou say'st,
    'Beauty is truth, truth beauty,'—that is all
      Ye know on earth, and all ye need to know.

JOHN KEATS

CHARITY

There is so much good in the worst of us,
And so much bad in the best of us,
That it ill behooves any of us
To find fault with the rest of us.

AUTHOR UNKNOWN

THE BARGAIN

My true love hath my heart, and I have his,
  By just exchange one for another given:
I hold his dear, and mine he cannot miss,
  There never was a better bargain driven:
    My true love hath my heart, and I have his.

His heart in me keeps him and me in one,
  My heart in him his thoughts and senses guides:
He loves my heart, for once it was his own,
  I cherish his because in me it bides:
    My true love hath my heart, and I have his.

SIR PHILIP SIDNEY

SONG

Come, rest in this bosom, my own stricken deer,
Though the herd have fled from thee, thy home is still
    here;
Here still is the smile, that no cloud can o'ercast,
And a heart and a hand all thy own to the last.

Oh! what was love made for, if 'tis not the same
Through joy and through torment, through glory and
    shame?
I know not, I ask not, if guilt's in that heart,
I but know that I love thee, whatever thou art.
Thou hast call'd me thy Angel in moments of bliss,
And thy Angel I'll be, 'mid the horrors of this,—
Through the furnace, unshrinking, thy steps to pursue,
And shield thee, and save thee,—or perish there too!

THOMAS MOORE

Love not me for comely grace,
　　For my pleasing eyes or face,
Nor for any outward part,
No, nor for a constant heart:
　　For these may fail or turn to ill,
　　　　So thou and I shall sever:
Keep, therefore, a true woman's eye,
And love me still but know not why—
　　So hast thou the same reason still
　　　　To dote upon me ever!

AUTHOR UNKNOWN

For God's sake hold your tongue, and let me love,
    Or chide my palsy, or my gout,
    My five grey hairs, or ruined fortune flout;
With wealth your state, your mind with arts improve,
       Take you a course, get you a place,
       Observe his Honor, or his Grace;
Or the king's real, or his stamped face
    Contemplate; what you will, approve,
    So you will let me love.

Alas, alas, who's injured by my love?
    What merchant's ships have my sighs drowned?
    Who says my tears have overflowed his ground?
When did my colds a forward spring remove?
       When did the heats which my veins fill
       Add one more to the plaguy bill?
Soldiers find wars, and lawyers find out still
    Litigious men, which quarrels move,
    Though she and I do love.

Call us what you will, we are made such by love;
    Call her one, me another fly,
    We're tapers too, and at our own cost die,
And we in us find the eagle and the dove
       The phoenix riddle hath more wit
       By us; we two being one are it.

So to one neutral thing both sexes fit,
    We die and rise the same, and prove
    Mysterious by this love.

We can die by it, if not live by love,
    And if unfit for tomb or hearse
    Our legend be, it will be fit for verse;
And if no piece of chronicle we prove,
        We'll build in sonnets pretty rooms;
        As well a well-wrought urn becomes
The greatest ashes, as half-acre tombs,
    And by these hymns all shall approve
    Us canonized for love.

And thus invoke us, "You, whom reverend love
    Made one another's hermitage;
    You, to whom love was peace, that now is rage:
Who did the whole world's soul contract, and drove
        Into the glasses of your eyes
        (So made such mirrors, and such spies,
That they did all to you epitomize);
    Countries, towns, courts beg from above
    A pattern of your love."

JOHN DONNE

In summer, when the days were long,
We walked together in the wood:
    Our heart was light, our step was strong;
Sweet flutterings were there in our blood,
    In summer, when the days were long.

We strayed from morn till evening came;
We gathered flowers, and wove us crowns;
    We walked mid poppies red as flame,
Or sat upon the yellow downs;
    And always wished our life the same.

In summer, when the days were long,
We leaped the hedgerow, crossed the brook;
    And still her voice flowed forth in song,
Or else she read some graceful book,
    In summer, when the days were long.

And then we sat beneath the trees,
With shadows lessening in the noon;
    And in the sunlight and the breeze,
We feasted, many a gorgeous June,
    While larks were singing o'er the leas.

In summer, when the days were long,
On dainty chicken, snow-white bread.
    We feasted, with no grace but song;

We plucked wild strawb'rries, ripe and red,
   In summer, when the days were long.

   We loved, and yet we knew it not,—
For loving seemed like breathing then;
   We found a heaven in every spot;
Saw angels, too, in all good men;
   And dreamed of God in grove and grot.

   In summer, when the days are long,
Alone I wander, muse alone.
   I see her not; but that old song
Under the fragrant wind is blown,
   In summer, when the days are long.

   Alone I wander in the wood:
But one fair spirit hears my sighs;
   And half I see, so glad and good,
The honest daylight of her eyes,
   That charmed me under earlier skies.

   In summer, when the days are long,
I love her as we loved of old.
   My heart is light, my step is strong;
For love brings back those hours of gold,
   In summer, when the days are long.

AUTHOR UNKNOWN

IF LOVE BE LOVE

In Love, if Love be Love, if Love be ours,
Faith and unfaith can ne'er be equal powers:
Unfaith in aught is want of faith in all.

It is the little rift within the lute,
That by and by will make the music mute,
And ever widening slowly silence all.

The little rift within the lover's lute
Or little pitted speck in garnered fruit,
That rotting inward slowly moulders all.

It is not worth the keeping: let it go:
But shall it? answer, darling, answer, no.
And trust me not at all or all in all.

ALFRED, LORD TENNYSON

Folk need a lot of loving in the morning;
  The day is all before, with cares beset—
The cares we know, and they that give no warning;
  For love is God's own antidote for fret.

Folk need a heap of loving at the noontime—
  In the battle lull, the moment snatched from
  strife—
Halfway between the waking and the croon time,
  While bickering and worriment are rife.

Folk hunger so for loving at the nighttime,
  When wearily they take them home to rest—
At slumber song and turning-out-the-light time—
  Of all the times for loving, that's the best.

Folk want a lot of loving every minute—
  The sympathy of others and their smile!
Till life's end, from the moment they begin it,
  Folks need a lot of loving all the while.

STRICKLAND GILLILAN

Give all to love;
Obey thy heart;
Friends, kindred, days,
Estate, good-fame,
Plans, credit, and the Muse—
Nothing refuse.

'Tis a brave master;
Let it have scope:
Follow it utterly,
Hope beyond hope:
High and more high
It dives into noon,
With wing unspent,
Untold intent;
But it is a god,
Knows its own path,
And the outlets of the sky.

It was not for the mean;
It requireth courage stout,
Souls above doubt,
Valor unbending;
Such 'twill reward—
They shall return
More than they were,
And ever ascending.

Leave all for love;
Yet, hear me, yet,
One word more thy heart behoved,
One pulse more of firm endeavor—
Keep thee today,
Tomorrow, forever,
Free as an Arab
Of thy beloved.

Cling with life to the maid;
But when the surprise,
First vague shadow of surmise
Flits across her bosom young
Of a joy apart from thee,
Free be she, fancy-free;
Nor thou detain her vesture's hem,
Nor the palest rose she flung
From her summer diadem.

Though thou loved her as thyself,
As a self of purer clay,
Though her parting dims the day,
Stealing grace from all alive;
Heartily know,
When half-gods go,
The gods arrive.

RALPH WALDO EMERSON

BELIEVE ME, IF ALL THOSE ENDEARING YOUNG CHARMS

Believe me, if all those endearing young charms,
    Which I gaze on so fondly today,
Were to change by tomorrow, and fleet in my arms,
    Like fairy-gifts fading away,
Thou wouldst still be adored, as this moment thou art,
    Let thy loveliness fade as it will,
And around the dear ruin each wish of my heart
    Would entwine itself verdantly still.

It is not while beauty and youth are thine own,
    And thy cheeks unprofaned by a tear,
That the fervour and faith of a soul can be known,
    To which time will but make thee more dear;
No, the heart that has truly loved never forgets,
    But as truly loves on to the close,
As the sunflower turns on her god, when he sets,
    The same look which she turned when he rose.

THOMAS MOORE

FORGIVEN

You left me when the weary weight of sorrow
 Lay, like a stone, upon my bursting heart;
It seemed as if no shimmering tomorrow
 Could dry the tears that you had caused to start.
You left me, never telling why you wandered—
 Without a word, without a last caress;
Left me with but the love that I had squandered,
 The husks of love and a vast loneliness.

And yet if you came back with arms stretched toward me,
 Came back tonight, with carefree, smiling eyes,
And said: "My journeying has somehow bored me,
 And love, though broken, never, never dies!"
I would forget the wounded heart you gave me,
 I would forget the bruises on my soul.
My old-time gods would rise again to save me;
 My dreams would grow supremely new and whole.

What though youth lay, a tattered garment, o'er you?
 Warm words would leap upon my lips, long dumb;
If you came back, with arms stretched out before you,
 And told me, dear, that you were glad to come!

MARGARET E. SANGSTER

MISS YOU

Miss you, miss you, miss you;
    Everything I do
Echoes with the laughter
    And the voice of You.

You're on every corner,
    Every turn and twist,
Every old familiar spot
    Whispers how you're missed.

Miss you, miss you, miss you!
    Everywhere I go
There are poignant memories
    Dancing in a row.

Silhouette and shadow
    Of your form and face,
Substance and reality
    Everywhere displace.

Oh, I miss you, miss you!
    God! I miss you, Girl!
There's a strange, sad silence
    'Mid the busy whirl,

Just as tho' the ordinary
    Daily things I do
Wait with me, expectant
    For a word from You.

Miss you, miss you, miss you!
    Nothing now seems true
Only that 'twas heaven
    Just to be with You.

DAVID CORY

THE INDIAN SERENADE

I arise from dreams of thee
In the first sweet sleep of night,
When the winds are breathing low,
And the stars are shining bright
I arise from dreams of thee,
And a spirit in my feet
Hath led me—who knows how?
To thy chamber window, Sweet!

The wandering airs they faint
On the dark, the silent stream—
The champak odors fail
Like sweet thoughts in a dream;
The nightingale's complaint,
It dies upon her heart;
As I must on thine,
Oh, beloved as thou art!

O lift me from the grass!
I die! I faint! I fail!
Let thy love in kisses rain
On my lips and eyelids pale.
My cheek is cold and white, alas!
My heart beats loud and fast;—
Oh! press it to thine own again,
Where it will break at last.

PERCY BYSSHE SHELLEY

I LOVE YOU

I love your lips when they're wet with wine
    And red with a wild desire;
I love your eyes when the lovelight lies
    Lit with a passionate fire.
I love your arms when the strands enmesh
    Your kisses against my face.

Not for me the cold, calm kiss
    Of a virgin's bloodless love;
Not for me the saint's white bliss,
    Nor the heart of a spotless dove.
But give me the love that so freely gives
    And laughs at the whole world's blame,
With your body so young and warm in my arms,
    It set my poor heart aflame.

So kiss me sweet with your warm wet mouth,
    Still fragrant with ruby wine,
And say with a fervor born of the South
    That your body and soul are mine.
Clasp me close in your warm young arms,
    While the pale stars shine above,
And we'll live our whole young lives away
    In the joys of a living love.

ELLA WHEELER WILCOX

Last night, ah, yesternight, betwixt her lips and mine
   There fell thy shadow, Cynara! thy breath was shed
Upon my soul between the kisses and the wine;
     And I was desolate and sick of an old passion,
    Yea, I was desolate and bowed my head:
     I have been faithful to thee, Cynara! in my fashion.

All night upon mine heart I felt her warm heart beat,
   Night-long within mine arms in love and sleep she lay;
Surely the kisses of her bought red mouth were sweet;
     But I was desolate and sick of an old passion,
    When I awoke and found the dawn was gray:
     I have been faithful to thee, Cynara! in my fashion.

I have forgot much, Cynara! gone with the wind,
   Flung roses, roses riotously with the throng,
Dancing, to put thy pale, lost lilies out of mind;
     But I was desolate and sick of an old passion,
    Yea, all the time, because the dance was long:
     I have been faithful to thee, Cynara! in my fashion.

I cried for madder music and for stronger wine,
   But when the feast is finished and the lamps expire,
Then falls thy shadow, Cynara! the night is thine;
     And I am desolate and sick of an old passion,
    Yea, hungry for the lips of my desire:
     I have been faithful to thee, Cynara! in my fashion.

ERNEST DOWSON

MY TRUE LOVE HATH MY HEART . . .

My true love hath my heart, and I have his,
By just exchange one for the other given.
I hold his dear, and mine he cannot miss;
There never was a better bargain driven.
His heart in me keeps me and him in one;
My heart in him his thoughts and senses guides;
He loves my heart, for once it was his own;
I cherish his, because in me it bides.
His heart his wound receivéd from my sight;
My heart was wounded with his wounded heart;
For as from me on him his hurt did light
So still methought in me his hurt did smart:
Both equal hurt, in this change sought our bliss;
My true love hath my heart, and I have his.

SIR PHILIP SIDNEY

Follow your saint, follow with accents sweet!
Haste you, sad notes, fall at her flying feet!
There, wrapped in cloud of sorrow, pity move,
And tell the ravisher of my soul I perish for her love:
But, if she scorns my never-ceasing pain,
Then burst with sighing in her sight and ne'er return
    again.

All that I sang still to her praise did tend,
Still she was first, still she my songs did end;
Yet she my love and music both doth fly,
The music that her echo is and beauty's sympathy.
Then let my notes pursue her scornful flight!
It shall suffice that they were breathed and died for
    her delight.

THOMAS CAMPION

Can life be a blessing
Or worth the possessing,
Can life be a blessing if love were away?
Ah no! though our love all night keep us waking,
And though he torment us with cares all the day,
Yet he sweetens, he sweetens our pains in the taking,
There's an hour at the last, there's an hour to repay.

In ev'ry possessing
The ravishing blessing,
In ev'ry possessing the fruit of our pain,
Poor lovers forget long ages of anguish,
Whate'er they have suffered and done to obtain;
'Tis a pleasure, a pleasure to sigh and to languish,
When we hope, when we hope to be happy again.

JOHN DRYDEN

I looked and saw your eyes
   In the shadow of your hair,
As a traveller sees the stream
   In the shadow of the wood;
And I said, "My faint heart sighs,
   Ah me! to linger there,
To drink deep and to dream
   In that sweet solitude."

I looked and saw your heart
   In the shadow of your eyes,
As a seeker sees the gold
   In the shadow of the stream;
And I said, "Ah me! what art
   Should win the immortal prize,
Whose want must make life cold
   And Heaven a hollow dream?"

I looked and saw your love
   In the shadow of your heart,
As a diver sees the pearl
   In the shadow of the sea;
And I murmured, not above
   My breath, but all apart,—
"Ah! you can love, true girl,
   And is your love for me?"

DANTE GABRIEL ROSSETTI

SHE WAS A PHANTOM OF DELIGHT

She was a phantom of delight
When first she gleamed upon my sight;
A lovely apparition, sent
To be a moment's ornament;
Her eyes as stars of twilight fair;
Like twilight's, too, her dusky hair;
But all things else about her drawn
From May-time and the cheerful dawn;
A dancing shape, an image gay,
To haunt, to startle and waylay.

I saw her upon nearer view,
A Spirit, yet a Woman too!
Her household motions light and free,
And steps of virgin liberty;
A countenance in which did meet
Sweet records, promises as sweet;
A creature not too bright or good
For human nature's daily food;
For transient sorrows, simple wiles,
Praise, blame, love, kisses, tears, and smiles.

And now I see with eye serene
The very pulse of the machine;
A being breathing thoughtful breath,
A traveller between life and death;

The reason firm, the temperate will,
Endurance, foresight, strength, and skill;
A perfect Woman, nobly planned,
To warn, to comfort, and command;
And yet a Spirit still, and bright
With something of angelic light.

WILLIAM WORDSWORTH

Camaraderie

If I knew you and you knew me—
    If both of us could clearly see,
And with an inner sight divine
    The meaning of your heart and mine—
I'm sure that we would differ less
    And clasp our hands in friendliness;
Our thoughts would pleasantly agree
    If I knew you and you knew me.

If I knew you and you knew me,
    As each one knows his own self, we
Could look each other in the face
    And see therein a truer grace.
Life has so many hidden woes,
    So many thorns for every rose;
The "why" of things our hearts would see,
    If I knew you and you knew me.

NIXON WATERMAN

THE KINDLY NEIGHBOR

I have a kindly neighbor, one who stands
Beside my gate and chats with me awhile.
Gives me the glory of his radiant smile
And comes at times to help with willing hands.
No station high or rank this man commands;
He, too, must trudge, as I, the long day's mile;
And yet, devoid of pomp or gaudy style,
He has a worth exceeding stocks or lands.

To him I go when sorrow's at my door;
On him I lean when burdens come my way;
Together oft we talk our trials o'er,
And there is warmth in each good night we say.
A kindly neighbor! Wars and strife shall end
When man has made the man next door his friend.

EDGAR A. GUEST

THE ONLY WAY TO HAVE A FRIEND

The only way to have a friend
  Is to be one yourself;
The only way to keep a friend
  Is to give from that wealth.

For friendship must be doublefold,
  Each one must give his share
Of feelings true if he would reap
  The blessings that are there.

If you would say, "He is my friend,"
  Then nothing else will do
But you must say, "I am his friend,"
  And prove that fact be true.

AUTHOR UNKNOWN

OUTWITTED

He drew a circle that shut me out—
Heretic, rebel, a thing to flout.
But Love and I hat the wit to win:
We drew a circle that took him in!

EDWIN MARKHAM

CONFIDE IN A FRIEND

When you're tired and worn at the close of day
And things just don't seem to be going your way,
When even your patience has come to an end,
Try taking time out and confide in a friend.

Perhaps he too may have walked the same road
With a much troubled heart and burdensome load,
To find peace and comfort somewhere near the end,
When he stopped long enough to confide in a friend.

For then are most welcome a few words of cheer,
For someone who willingly lends you an ear.
No troubles exist that time cannot mend,
But to get quick relief, just confide in a friend.

AUTHOR UNKNOWN

TO MY FRIEND

I have never been rich before,
    But you have poured
Into my heart's high door
    A golden hoard.

My wealth is the vision shared,
    The sympathy,
The feast of the soul prepared
    By you for me.

Together we wander through
    The wooded ways.
Old beauties are green and new
    Seen through your gaze.

I look for no greater prize
    Than your soft voice.
The steadiness of your eyes
    Is my heart's choice.

I have never been rich before,
    But I divine
Your step on my sunlit floor
    And wealth is mine!

ANNE CAMPBELL

There is always a place for you at my table,
    You never need to be invited.
I'll share every crust as long as I'm able,
    And know you will be delighted.
There is always a place for you by my fire,
    And though it may burn to embers,
If warmth and good cheer are your desire
    The friend of your heart remembers!
There is always a place for you by my side,
    And should the years tear us apart,
I will face lonely moments more satisfied
    With a place for you in my heart!

ANNE CAMPBELL

Around the corner I have a friend,
In this great city that has no end;
Yet days go by, and weeks rush on,
And before I know it a year is gone,
And I never see my old friend's face,
For Life is a swift and terrible race.
He knows I like him just as well
As in the days when I rang his bell
And he rang mine. We were younger then,
And now we are busy, tired men:
Tired with trying to make a name.
"Tomorrow," I say, "I will call on Jim,
Just to show that I'm thinking of him."

But tomorrow comes—and tomorrow goes,
And the distance between us grows and grows
Around the corner! —yet miles away. . . .
"Here's a telegram, sir. . . ."
   Jim died today."
And that's what we get, and deserve in the end:
Around the corner, a vanished friend.

CHARLES HANSON TOWNE

Friendship needs no studied phrases,
    Polished face, or winning wiles;
Friendship deals no lavish praises,
    Friendship dons no surface smiles.

Friendship follows Nature's diction,
    Shuns the blandishments of Art,
Boldly severs truth from fiction,
    Speaks the language of the heart.

Friendship favors no condition,
    Scorns a narrow-minded creed,
Lovingly fulfills its mission,
    Be it word or be it deed.

Friendship cheers the faint and weary,
    Makes the timid spirit brave,
Warns the erring, lights the dreary,
    Smooths the passage to the grave.

Friendship—pure, unselfish friendship,
    All through life's allotted span,
Nurtures, strengthens, widens, lengthens,
    Man's relationship with man.

AUTHOR UNKNOWN

I'M NOBODY! WHO ARE YOU?

I'm Nobody! Who are you?
Are you—Nobody—Too?
Then there's a pair of us?
Don't tell! they'd advertise—you know!

How dreary—to be—Somebody!
How public—like a Frog—
To tell one's name—the livelong June—
To an admiring Bog!

EMILY DICKINSON

FORBEARANCE

Hast thou named all the birds without a gun?
Loved the wood-rose, and left it on its stalk?
At rich men's tables eaten bread and pulse?
Unarmed, faced danger with a heart of trust?
And loved so well a high behavior,
In man or maid, that thou from speech refrained,
Nobility more nobly to repay?
O, be my friend, and teach me to be thine!

RALPH WALDO EMERSON

Character

ODE TO SOLITUDE

Happy the man, whose wish and care
    A few paternal acres bound,
Content to breathe his native air,
        In his own ground.

Whose herds with milk, whose fields with bread,
    Whose flocks supply him with attire;
Whose trees in summer yield him shade,
        In winter, fire.

Blest who can unconcern'dly find
    Hours, days, and years slide soft away
In health of body, peace of mind,
        Quiet by day,

Sound sleep by night; study and ease
    Together mixt; sweet recreation,
And Innocence, which most does please
        With meditation.

Thus let me live, unseen, unknown;
    Thus unlamented let me die;
Steal from the world, and not a stone
        Tell where I lie.

ALEXANDER POPE

INVICTUS

Out of the night that covers me,
    Black as the Pit from pole to pole,
I thank whatever gods may be
    For my unconquerable soul.

In the fell clutch of circumstance
    I have not winced nor cried aloud.
Under the bludgeonings of chance
    My head is bloody, but unbowed.

Beyond this place of wrath and tears
    Looms but the horror of the shade,
And yet the menace of the years
    Finds, and shall find me, unafraid.

It matters not how strait the gate,
    How charged with punishments the scroll,
I am the master of my fate:
    I am the captain of my soul.

WILLIAM ERNEST HENLEY

Erasers are the nicest things!
  Of that there is no doubt.
We write wrong words. A few quick swipes—
  And big mistakes fade out.
And you will find erasers,
  Of a very different kind,
Extremely helpful, if you will try
  To bear these facts in mind:
When you bump someone in a crowd,
  And almost knock her down,
A soft "I'm sorry!" may bring smiles
  And rub out that old frown.
Apologies, invariably,
  Obliterate mistakes;
And three small words, "I love you!"
  Can erase the worst heartaches.

AUTHOR UNKNOWN

Let me today do something that will take
  A little sadness from the world's vast store,
And may I be so favored as to make
  Of joy's too scanty sum a little more.

Let me not hurt, by any selfish deed
  Or thoughtless word, the heart of foe or friend.
Nor would I pass unseeing worthy need,
  Or sin by silence when I should defend.

However meager be my worldly wealth,
  Let me give something that shall aid my kind—
A word of courage, or a thought of health
  Dropped as I pass for troubled hearts to find.

Let me tonight look back across the span
  'Twixt dawn and dark, and to my conscience say—
Because of some good act to beast or man—
  "The world is better that I lived today."

ELLA WHEELER WILCOX

SUCCESS

If you want a thing bad enough
To go out and fight for it,
Work day and night for it,
Give up your time and your peace and your sleep for it
If only desire of it
Makes you quite mad enough
Never to tire of it,
Makes you hold all other things tawdry and cheap for it
If life seems all empty and useless without it
And all that you scheme and you dream is about it,
If gladly you'll sweat for it,
Fret for it,
Plan for it,
Lose all your terror of God or man for it,
If you'll simply go after that thing that you want,
With all your capacity,
Strength and sagacity,
Faith, hope and confidence, stern pertinacity,
If neither cold poverty, famished and gaunt,
Nor sickness nor pain
Of body or brain
Can turn you away from the thing that you want,
If dogged and grim you besiege and beset it,
    You'll get it!

BERTON BRALEY

WATCH YOURSELF GO BY

Just stand aside and watch yourself go by;
Think of yourself as "he" instead of "I."
Note closely as in other men you note
The bag-kneed trousers and the seedy coat.
Pick flaws; find fault; forget the man is you,
And strive to make your estimate ring true.
Confront yourself and look you in the eye—
Just stand aside and watch yourself go by.

Interpret all your motives just as though
You looked on one whose aims you did not know.
Let undisguised contempt surge through you when
You see you shirk, O commonest of men!
Despise your cowardice; condemn whate'er
You note of falseness in you anywhere.
Defend not one defect that shares your eye—
Just stand aside and watch yourself go by.

And then, with eyes unveiled to what you loathe,
To sins that with sweet charity you'd clothe,
Back to your self-walled tenement you'll go
With tolerance for all who dwell below.
The faults of others then will dwarf and shrink,
Love's chain grows stronger by one mighty link,
When you, with "he" as substitute for "I,"
Have stood aside and watched yourself go by.

STRICKLAND GILLILAN

A VOW FOR NEW YEAR'S

Every hour and every minute
Has a New Year's Day tucked in it
And each single one of these
Is packed with possibilities—
Possibilities of pleasure,
Of sharing with some friend some treasure,
Of making a "Good morning" cheery—
Making a good one from a dreary—
Of shutting tight the lips to hide
A bit of gossip safe inside
Instead of letting it get out
To roam about and maybe do
More harm than you would like it to.
Let us take a little vow,
Since it is the New Year now,
To be more kind, more brave, more gay
This year and make each single day
That comes a model New Year's Day!

MARY CAROLYN DAVIES

WE WILL SPEAK OUT

We will speak out, we will be heard,
 Though all earth's systems crack;
We will not bate a single word,
 Nor take a letter back.
Let liars fear, let cowards shrink,
 Let traitors turn away;
Whatever we have dared to think
 That dare we also say.
We speak the truth, and what care we
 For hissing and for scorn,
While some faint gleamings we can see
 Of Freedom's coming morn?

JAMES RUSSELL LOWELL

THE CHARACTER OF A HAPPY LIFE

How happy is he born and taught
   That serveth not another's will;
Whose armour is his honest thought,
   And simple truth his utmost skill;

Whose passions not his masters are;
   Whose soul is still prepared for death,
Untied unto the world by care
   Of public fame or private breath;

Who envies none that chance doth raise,
   Nor vice; who never understood
How deepest wounds are given by praise;
   Nor rules of state, but rules of good;

Who hath his life from rumours freed;
   Whose conscience is his strong retreat;
Whose state can neither flatterers feed,
   Nor ruin make oppressors great;

Who God doth late and early pray
   More of his grace than gifts to lend;
And entertains the harmless day
   With a religious book or friend.

This man is free from servile bands
    Of hope to rise or fear to fall:
Lord of himself, though not of lands,
    And, having nothing, yet hath all.

SIR HENRY WOOTTON

Faith

Glory be to God for dappled things—
      For skies of couple-colour as a brinded cow;
    For rose-moles all in stipple upon trout that
   swim;
Fresh-firecoal chestnut-falls; finches' wings;
   Landscape plotted and pieced—fold, fallow,
        and plough;
     And all trades, their gear and tackle and trim.

All things counter, original, spare, strange;
   Whatever is fickle, freckled (who knows how?)
     With swift, slow; sweet, sour; adazzle, dim;
He fathers-forth whose beauty is past change:
     Praise him.

GERARD MANLEY HOPKINS

Say not the struggle naught availeth,
    The labour and the wounds are vain,
The enemy faints not, nor faileth,
    And as things have been they remain.

If hopes were dupes, fears may be liars;
    It may be, in yon smoke conceal'd,
Your comrades chase e'en now the fliers,
    And, but for you, possess the field.

For while the tired waves, vainly breaking,
    Seem here no painful inch to gain,
Far back, through creeks and inlets making,
    Comes silent, flooding in, the main.

And not by eastern windows only,
    When daylight comes, comes in the light;
In front the sun climbs slow, how slowly!
    But westward, look, the land is bright!

ARTHUR HUGH CLOUGH

SONG

Go and catch a falling star,
    Get with child a mandrake root,
Tell me where all past years are,
    Or who cleft the Devil's foot;
Teach me to hear mermaids singing,
Or to keep off envy's stinging,
      And find
      What wind
Serves to advance an honest mind.

If thou be'st born to strange sights,
    Things invisible to see,
Ride ten thousand days and nights
    Till Age snow white hairs on thee;
Thou, when thou return'st, wilt tell me
All strange wonders that befell thee,
      And swear
      No where
Lives a woman true and fair.

If thou find'st one, let me know;
    Such a pilgrimage were sweet.
Yet do not; I would not go,
    Though at next door we might meet.

Though she were true when you met her,
And last till you write your letter,
      Yet she
      Will be
False, ere I come, to two or three.

JOHN DONNE

IT MIGHT HAVE BEEN WORSE

Sometimes I pause and sadly think
    Of the things that might have been,
Of the golden chances I let slip by,
    And which never returned again.

Think of the joys that might have been mine;
    The prizes I almost won,
The goals I missed by a mere hair's breadth;
    And the things I might have done.

It fills me with gloom when I ponder thus,
    Till I look on the other side,
How I might have been completely engulfed
    By misfortune's surging tide.

The unknown dangers lurking about,
    Which I passed safely through
The evils and sorrows that I've been spared
    Pass plainly now in review.

So when I am downcast and feeling sad,
    I repeat over and over again,
Things are far from being as bad
    As they easily might have been.

G.J. RUSSELL

I HAVE FOUND SUCH JOY

I have found such joy in simple things;
    A plain, clean room, a nut-brown loaf of bread,
A cup of milk, a kettle as it sings,
    The shelter of a roof above my head,
And in a leaf-laced square along the floor,
Where yellow sunlight glimmers through a door.

I have found such joy in things that fill
    My quiet days: a curtain's blowing grace,
A potted plant upon my window sill,
    A rose, fresh-cut and placed within a vase;
A table cleared, a lamp beside a chair,
And books I long have loved beside me there.

Oh, I have found such joys I wish I might
    Tell every woman who goes seeking far
For some elusive, feverish delight,
    That very close to home the great joys are:
The elemental things—old as the race,
Yet never, through the ages, commonplace.

GRACE NOLL CROWELL

EQUIPMENT

Figure it out for yourself, my lad,
You've all that the greatest of men have had,
Two arms, two hands, two legs, two eyes
And brain to use if you would be wise.
With this equipment they all began,
So start for the top and say, "I can."

Look them over, the wise and great,
They take their food from a common plate,
And similar knives and forks they use,
With similar laces they tie their shoes,
The world considers them brave and smart,
But you've all they had when they made their start.

You can triumph and come to skill,
You can be great if you only will.
You're well equipped for what fight you choose,
You have legs and arms and a brain to use,
And the man who has risen great deeds to do
Began his life with no more than you.

You are the handicap you must face,
You are the one who must choose your place,
You must say where you want to go,
How much you will study the truth to know.
God has equipped you for life, but He
Lets you decide what you want to be.

Courage must come from the soul within,
The man must furnish the will to win.
So figure it out for yourself, my lad.
You were born with all that the great have had,
With your equipment they all began
Get hold of yourself, and say: *"I can."*

EDGAR A. GUEST

This prayer I make,
Knowing that Nature never did betray
The heart that loved her; 'tis her privilege,
Through all the years of this our life, to lead
From joy to joy: for she can so inform
The mind that is within us, so impress
With quietness and beauty, and so feed
With lofty thoughts, that neither evil tongues,
Rash judgments, nor the sneers of selfish men,
Nor greetings where no kindness is, nor all
The dreary intercourse of daily life,
Shall e'er prevail against us, or disturb
Our cheerful faith, that all which we behold
Is full of blessings.

WILLIAM WORDSWORTH

A SMILE

A smile costs nothing but gives much—
It takes but a moment, but the memory of it usually lasts
    forever.
None are so rich that can get along without it—
And none are so poor but that can be made rich by it.
It enriches those who receive
Without making poor those who give—
It creates sunshine in the home,
Fosters good will in business
And is the best antidote for trouble—
And yet it cannot be begged, borrowed or stolen, for it is of
    no value
Unless it is freely given away.
Some people are too busy to give you a smile—
Give them one of yours—
For the good Lord knows that no one needs a smile so badly
As he or she who has no more smiles left to give.

AUTHOR UNKNOWN

"All honor to him, who shall win the fight,"
The world has cried for a thousand years,
But to him who tries and who fails and dies,
I give great honor and glory and tears;
Give glory and honor and pitiful tears
To all who fail in their deeds sublime;
Their ghosts are many in the van of years,
They were born with time in advance of time.
Oh! great is the hero who wins a name,
But greater many and many a time
Some pale-faced fellow who dies in shame
And lets God publish the thought sublime,
And great is the man with the sword undrawn,
And good is the man who refrains from wine,
But the man who fails and yet still fights on,
Lo, he is a twin brother of mine.

JOAQUIN MILLER

LET US HAVE PEACE

The earth is weary of our foolish wars.
Her hills and shores were shaped for lovely things,
Yet all our years are spent in bickerings
  Beneath the astonished stars.

April by April laden with beauty comes,
Autumn by Autumn turns our toil to gain,
But hand at sword hilt, still we start and strain
  To catch the beat of drums.

Knowledge to knowledge adding, skill to skill,
We strive for others' good as for our own—
And then, like cavemen snarling with a bone,
  We turn and rend and kill. . . .

With life so fair, and all too short a lease
Upon our special star! Nay, love and trust,
Not blood and thunder shall redeem our dust.
  Let us have peace!

NANCY BYRD TURNER

I sought to hear the voice of God,
   And climbed the topmost steeple.
But God declared: "Go down again,
   I dwell among the people."

LOUIS I. NEWMAN

RING OUT, WILD BELLS

Ring out, wild bells, to the wild sky,
    The flying cloud, the frosty light:
    The year is dying in the night;
Ring out, wild bells, and let him die.

Ring out the old, ring in the new,
    Ring, happy bells, across the snow:
    The year is going, let him go;
Ring out the false, ring in the true.

ALFRED, LORD TENNYSON

A THING OF BEAUTY

A thing of beauty is a joy for ever:
Its loveliness increases; it will never
Pass into nothingness; but still will keep
A bower quiet for us, and a sleep
Full of sweet dreams, and health, and quiet breathing.
Therefore, on every morrow, are we wreathing
A flowery band to bind us to the earth,
Spite of despondence, of the inhuman dearth
Of noble natures, of the gloomy days,
Of all the unhealthy and o'er-darkened ways
Made for our searching: yes, in spite of all,
Some shape of beauty moves away the pall
From our dark spirits.

JOHN KEATS

THERE IS NO DEATH

There is no death! The stars go down
   To rise upon some other shore,
And bright in heaven's jeweled crown
   They shine for evermore.

There is no death! The dust we tread
   Shall change beneath the summer showers
To golden grain or mellow fruit
   Or rainbow-tinted flowers.

There is no death! The leaves may fall,
   The flowers may fade and pass away—
They only wait, through wintry hours,
   The coming of the May.

The bird-like voice, whose joyous tones
   Made glad this scene of sin and strife,
Sings now an everlasting song
   Amid the tree of life.

And ever near us, though unseen,
   The dear immortal spirits tread;
For all the boundless universe
   Is Life—there are no dead!

JOHN LUCKEY McCREERY

FLEURETTE

My leg? It's off at the knee.
Do I miss it? Well, some. You see
I've had it since I was born;
And lately a devilish corn.
(I rather chuckle with glee
To think how I've fooled that corn.)

But I'll hobble around all right.
It isn't that, it's my face.
Oh I know I'm a hideous sight,
Hardly a thing in place;
Sort of gargoyle, you'd say.
Nurse won't give me a glass,
But I see the folks as they pass
Shudder and turn away;
Turn away in distress . . .
Mirror enough, I guess.

I'm gay! You bet I *am* gay;
But I wasn't a while ago.
If you'd seen me even to-day,
The darndest picture of woe,
With this Caliban mug of mine,
So ravaged and raw and red,
Turned to the wall—in fine,
Wishing that I was dead. . . .

So over the blanket's rim
I raised my terrible face,
And I saw—how I envied him!
A girl of such delicate grace;
Sixteen, all laughter and love;
As gay as a linnet, and yet
As tenderly sweet as a dove;
Half woman, half child—Fleurette.

What has happened since then,
Since I lay with my face to the wall,
The most despairing of men?
Listen! I'll tell you all.
That *poilu* across the way,
With the shrapnel wound in his head,
Has a sister: she came to day
To sit awhile by his bed.
All morning I heard him fret:
"Oh, when will she come, Fleurette?"

Then sudden, a joyous cry;
The tripping of little feet;
The softest, tenderest sigh;
A voice so fresh and sweet;
Clear as a silver bell,
Fresh as the morning dews:

"*C'est toi, c'est toi, Marcel!*
Mon frère, comme je suis heureuse!"

Then I turned to the wall again.
(I was awfully blue, you see,)
And I thought with a bitter pain:
"Such visions are not for me."

So there like a log I lay,
All hidden, I thought, from view,
When sudden I heard her say:
"Ah! Who is that *malheureux?*"

Then briefly I heard him tell
(However he came to know)
How I'd smothered a bomb that fell
Into the trench, and so
None of my men were hit,
Though it busted me up a bit.

Well, I didn't quiver an eye,
And he chattered and there she sat;
And I fancied I heard her sigh—
But I wouldn't just swear to that.
And maybe she wasn't so bright,
Though she talked in a merry strain,
And I closed my eyes ever so tight,

Yet I saw her ever so plain:
Her dear little tilted nose,
Her delicate, dimpled chin,
Her mouth like a budding rose,
And the glistening pearls within;
Her eyes like the violet:
Such a rare little queen—Fleurette.

And at last when she rose to go,
The light was a little dim,
And I ventured to peep, and so
I saw her, graceful and slim,
And she kissed him and kissed him, and oh
How I envied and envied him!

So when she was gone I said
In rather a dreary voice
To him of the opposite bed:
"Ah, friend, how you must rejoice!
But me, I'm a thing of dread.
For me nevermore the bliss,
The thrill of a woman's kiss."

Then I stopped, for lo! she was there,
And a great light shone in her eyes.
And me! I could only stare,
I was taken so by surprise,

When gently she bent her head:
"*May I kiss you, Sergeant?*" she said.

Then she kissed my burning lips
With her mouth like a scented flower,
And I thrilled to the finger-tips,
And I hadn't even the power
To say: "God bless you, dear!"
And I felt such a precious tear
Fall on my withered cheek,
And darn it! I couldn't speak.
And so she went sadly away,
And I knew that my eyes were wet.
Ah, not to my dying day
Will I forget, forget!
Can you wonder now I am gay?
God bless her, that little Fleurette!

ROBERT SERVICE

IT CAN BE DONE

The man who misses all the fun
Is he who says, "It can't be done."
In solemn pride he stands aloof
And greets each venture with reproof.
Had he the power he'd efface
The history of the human race;
We'd have no radio or motor cars,
No streets lit by electric stars;
No telegraph nor telephone,
We'd linger in the age of stone.
The world would sleep if things were run
By men who say, "It can't be done."

AUTHOR UNKNOWN

DEFEAT

No one is beat till he quits,
    No one is through till he stops,
No matter how hard Failure hits,
    No matter how often he drops,
A fellow's not down till he lies
In the dust and refuses to rise.

Fate can slam him and bang him around,
    And batter his frame till he's sore,
But she never can say that he's downed
    While he bobs up serenely for more.
A fellow's not dead till he dies,
Nor beat till no longer he tries.

EDGAR GUEST

YOU MUSTN'T QUIT

When things go wrong, as they sometimes will,
When the road you're trudging seems all uphill,
When the funds are low and the debts are high
And you want to smile, but you have to sigh,
When care is pressing you down a bit,
Rest! if you must—but never quit.

Life is queer, with its twists and turns,
As every one of us sometimes learns,
And many a failure turns about
When he might have won if he'd stuck it out;
Stick to your task, though the pace seems slow—
You may succeed with one more blow.

Success is failure turned inside out—
The silver tint of the clouds of doubt—
And you never can tell how close you are,
It may be near when it seems afar;
So stick to the fight when you're hardest hit—
It's when things seem worst that YOU MUSTN'T QUIT.

AUTHOR UNKNOWN

BLESS THIS HOUSE

Bless this house, O Lord, we pray
Make it safe by night and day:
Bless these walls so firm and stout
Keeping want and trouble out;

Bless the roof and chimneys tall,
Let Thy peace lie over all:
Bless this door, that it may prove
Ever open to joy and love.

Bless these windows shining bright,
Letting in God's heavenly light:
Bless the hearth ablazing there,
With smoke ascending like a prayer:

Bless the people here within,
Keep them pure and free from sin;
Bless us all that we may be
Fit, O Lord, to dwell with thee.

MARY H. BRAHE AND HELEN TAYLOR

MY PRAYER

Great God, I ask thee for no meaner pelf
Than that I may not disappoint myself;
That in my action I may soar as high
As I can now discern with this clear eye.

And next in value, which thy kindness lends,
That I may greatly disappoint my friends,
Howe'er they think or hope that it may be,
They may not dream how thou'st distinguished me;

That my weak hand may equal my firm faith,
And my life practice more than my tongue saith;
    That my low conduct may not show,
        Nor my relenting lines,
    That I thy purpose did not know,
        Or overrated thy designs.

HENRY DAVID THOREAU

Oh, love this house, and make of it a Home—
A cherished, hallowed place.
Root roses at its base, and freely paint
The glow of welcome on its smiling face!
For after friends are gone, and children marry,
And you are left alone . . .
The house you loved will clasp you to its heart,
Within its arms of lumber and of stone.

ROSA ZAGNONI MARINONI

God of our fathers, known of old—
    Lord of our far-flung battle-line—
Beneath whose awful Hand we hold
    Dominion over palm and pine—
Lord God of Hosts, be with us yet,
Lest we forget, lest we forget!

The tumult and the shouting dies—
    The captains and the kings depart—
Still stands Thine ancient sacrifice,
    An humble and a contrite heart.
Lord God of Hosts, be with us yet,
Lest we forget, lest we forget!

Far-call'd our navies melt away—
    On dune and headland sinks the fire—
Lo, all our pomp of yesterday
    Is one with Nineveh and Tyre!
Judge of the Nations, spare us yet,
Lest we forget, lest we forget!

If, drunk with sight of power, we loose
    Wild tongues that have not Thee in awe—
Such boasting as the Gentiles use
    Or lesser breeds without the Law—
Lord God of Hosts, be with us yet,
Lest we forget, lest we forget!

For heathen heart that puts her trust
    In reeking tube and iron shard—
All valiant dust that builds on dust,
    And guarding calls not Thee to guard—
For frantic boast and foolish word,
Thy Mercy on Thy People, Lord!

RUDYARD KIPLING

If you are on the Gloomy Line,
    Get a transfer.
If you're inclined to fret and pine,
    Get a transfer.
Get off the track of doubt and gloom,
Get on the Sunshine Track—there's room—
    Get a transfer.

If you're on the Worry Train,
    Get a transfer.
You must not stay there and complain,
    Get a transfer.
The Cheerful Cars are passing through,
And there's lots of room for you—
    Get a transfer.
If you're on the Grouchy Track,
    Get a transfer.
Just take a Happy Special back,
    Get a transfer.
Jump on the train and pull the rope,
That lands you at the station Hope—
    Get a transfer.

AUTHOR UNKNOWN

EVERYONE SANG

Everyone suddenly burst out singing;
And I was fill'd with such delight
As prison'd birds must find in freedom
Winging wildly across the white
Orchards and dark-green fields; on; on; and out of sight.

Everyone's voice was suddenly lifted,
And beauty came like the setting sun.
My heart was shaken with tears; and horror
Drifted away . . . O but every one
Was a bird; and the song was wordless; the singing will
    never be done.

SIEGFRIED SASSOON

Nature

When the frost is on the punkin and the fodder's in the
    shock,
And you hear the kyouck and gobble of the struttin'
    turkey-cock,
And the clackin' of the guineys, and the cluckin' of the
    hens,
And the rooster's hallylooyer as he tiptoes on the fence;
Oh, it's then's the times a feller is a-feelin' at his best,
With the risin' sun to greet him from a night of peaceful
    rest,
As he leaves the house, bareheaded, and goes out to feed
    the stock,
When the frost is on the punkin and the fodder's in the
    shock.

They's something kind o'harty-like about the atmusfere
When the heat of summer's over and the coolin' fall is
    here.—
Of course we miss the flowers, and the blossoms on the
    trees,
And the mumble of the hummin'-birds and buzzin' of
    the bees;
But the air's so appetizin', and the landscape through
    the haze
Of a crisp and sunny morning of the airly autumn days
Is a pictur' that no painter has the colorin' to mock,—

When the frost is on the punkin and the fodder's in the
    shock.
The husky, rusty russel of the tossels of the corn,
And the raspin' of the tangled leaves, as golden as the
    morn;
The stubble in the furries—kind o' lonesome-like, but
    still
A-preachin' sermuns to us of the barns they growed to
    fill;
The straw-stack in the medder, and the reaper in the
    shed;
The hosses in theyr stalls below, the clover overhead,—
Oh, it sets my hart a-clickin' like the tickin' of a clock,
When the frost is on the punkin and the fodder's in the
    shock!

Then your apples all is gethered, and the ones a feller
    keeps
Is poured around the celler-floor in red and yeller heaps;
And your cider-makin' 's over, and your wimmern-folks is
    through
With their mince and apple butter, and theyr souse and
    saussage, too!. . . .
I don't know how to tell it—but ef sich a thing could be
As the Angels wantin' boardin', and they'd call around
    on *me*—

I'd want to 'commodate 'em—all the whole-indurin'
    flock—
When the frost is on the punkin and the fodder's in
    the shock!

JAMES WHITCOMB RILEY

There is a pleasure in the pathless woods,
There is a rapture on the lonely shore,
There is society where none intrudes
By the deep sea, and music in its roar:
I love not man the less, but nature more,
From these our interviews, in which I steal
From all I may be, or have been before,
To mingle with the universe, and feel
What I can ne'er express, yet cannot all conceal.

Roll on, thou deep and dark blue Ocean,—roll!
Ten thousand fleets sweep over thee in vain;
Man marks the earth with ruin,—his control
Stops with the shore;—upon the watery plain
The wrecks are all thy deed, nor doth remain
A shadow of man's ravage, save his own,
When, for a moment, like a drop of rain,
He sinks into thy depths with bubbling groan,
Without a grave, unknelled, uncoffined, and unknown.

His steps are not upon thy paths,—thy fields
Are not a spoil for him,—thou dost arise
And shake him from thee; the vile strength he wields
For earth's destruction thou dost all despise,
Spurning him from thy bosom to the skies,
And send'st him, shivering in thy playful spray

And howling, to his gods, where haply lies
   His petty hope in some near port or bay,
And dashest him again to earth:—there let him lay.

   The armaments which thunderstrike the walls
   Of rock-built cities, bidding nations quake
   And monarchs tremble in their capitals,
   The oak leviathans, whose huge ribs make
   Their clay creator the vain title take
   Of lord of thee and arbiter of war,—
   These are thy toys, and, as the snowy flake,
   They melt into thy yeast of waves, which mar
Alike the Armada's pride or spoils of Trafalgar.

   Thy shores are empires, changed in all save thee;
   Assyria, Greece, Rome, Carthage, what are they?
   Thy waters wasted them while they were free,
   And many a tyrant since; their shores obey
   The stranger, slave, or savage; their decay
   Has dried up realms to deserts: not so thou;
   Unchangeable save to thy wild waves' play,
   Time writes no wrinkles on thine azure brow;
Such as creation's dawn beheld, thou rollest now.

   Thou glorious mirror, where the Almighty's form
   Glasses itself in tempests; in all time,
   Calm or convulsed,—in breeze, or gale, or storm,

Icing the pole, or in the torrid clime
Dark-heaving; boundless, endless, and sublime,
The image of Eternity,—the throne
Of the Invisible! even from out thy slime
The monsters of the deep are made; each zone
Obeys thee; thou goest forth, dread, fathomless, alone.

And I have loved thee, Ocean! and my joy
Of youthful sports was on thy breast to be
Borne, like thy bubbles, onward; from a boy
I wantoned with thy breakers,—they to me
Were a delight; and if the freshening sea
Made them a terror, 't was a pleasing fear;
For I was as it were a child of thee,
And trusted to thy billows far and near,
And laid my hand upon thy mane,—as I do here.

GEORGE GORDON, LORD BYRON

NIGHTINGALES

Beautiful must be the mountains whence ye come,
And bright in the fruitful valleys the streams, wherefrom
    Ye learn your song:
Where are those starry woods? O might I wander there,
  Among the flowers, which in that heavenly air
    Bloom the year long!

Nay, barren are those mountains and spent the streams:
Our song is the voice of desire, that haunts our dreams,
    A throe of the heart,
Whose pining visions dim, forbidden hopes profound,
  No dying cadence nor long sigh can sound,
    For all our art.

Alone, aloud in the raptured ear of men
We pour our dark nocturnal secret; and then,
    As night is withdrawn
From these sweet-springing meads and bursting boughs of
    May,
  Dream, while the innumerable choir of day
    Welcome the dawn.

ROBERT BRIDGES

A DESCRIPTION OF A CITY SHOWER

Careful observers may foretell the hour
(By sure prognostics) when to dread a shower.
While rain depends, the pensive cat gives o'er
Her frolics, and pursues her tail no more.
Returning home at night, you'll find the sink
Strike your offended sense with double stink.
If you be wise, then go not far to dine;
You'll spend in coach-hire more than save in wine.
A coming shower your shooting corns presage,
Old aches throb, your hollow tooth will rage:
Sauntering in coffee-house is Dulman seen;
He damns the climate and complains of spleen.

    Meanwhile the South, rising with dabbled wings,
A sable cloud athwart the welkin flings,
That swilled more liquor than it could contain,
And, like a drunkard, gives it up again.
Brisk Susan whips her linen from the rope,
While the first drizzling shower is borne aslope:
Such is that sprinkling which some careless quean
Flirts on you from her mop, but not so clean:
You fly, invoke the gods; then turning, stop
To rail; she singing, still whirls on her mop.
Nor yet the dust had shunned the unequal strife,
But, aided by the wind, fought still for life,
And wafted with its foe by violent gust,
'Twas doubtful which was rain and which was dust.

Ah! where must needy poet seek for aid,
When dust and rain at once his coat invade?
Sole coat, where dust cemented by the rain
Erects the nap, and leaves a cloudy stain.

Now in contiguous drops the flood comes down,
Threatening with deluge this devoted town.
To shops in crowds the daggled females fly,
Pretend to cheapen goods, but nothing buy.
The Templar spruce, while every spout's abroach,
Stays till 'tis fair, yet seems to call a coach.
The tucked-up sempstress walks with hasty strides,
While streams run down her oiled umbrella's sides.
Here various kinds, by various fortunes led,
Commence acquaintance underneath a shed.
Triumphant Tories and desponding Whigs
Forget their feuds, and join to save their wigs.
Boxed in a chair the beau impatient sits,
While spouts run clattering o'er the roof by fits;
And ever and anon with frightful din
The leather sounds; he trembles from within.
So when Troy chairmen bore the wooden steed,
Pregnant with Greeks impatient to be freed
(Those bully Greeks, who, as the moderns do,
Instead of paying chairmen, run them through),
Laocoön struck the outside with his spear,
And each imprisoned hero quaked for fear.

Now from all parts the swelling kennels flow,
And bear their trophies with them as they go:
Filth of all hues and odours seem to tell
What street they sailed from, by their sight and smell.
They, as each torrent drives with rapid force,
From Smithfield or St. Pulchre's shape their course,
And in huge confluence joined at Snow Hill ridge,
Fall from the conduit prone to Holborn Bridge.
Sweepings from butchers' stalls, dung, guts, and blood,
Drowned puppies, stinking sprats, all drenched in
    mud,
Dead cats, and turnip-tops, come tumbling down
    the flood.

JONATHAN SWIFT

I must go down to the seas again, to the lonely sea and
    the sky,
And all I ask is a tall ship and a star to steer her by,
And the wheel's kick and the wind's song and the
    white sail's shaking,
And a gray mist on the sea's face and a gray dawn
    breaking.

I must go down to the seas again, for the call of the
    running tide
Is a wild call and a clear call that may not be denied;
And all I ask is a windy day with the white clouds fly-
    ing,
And the flung spray and the blown spume, and the
    sea-gulls crying.

I must go down to the seas again to the vagrant gypsy
    life.
To the gull's way and the whale's way where the wind's
    like a whetted knife;
And all I ask is a merry yarn from a laughing fellow-
    rover,
And quiet sleep and a sweet dream when the long
    trick's over.

JOHN MASEFIELD

Apparently with no surprise
To any happy Flower
The Frost beheads it at its play—
In accidental power—
The blonde Assassin passes on—
The Sun proceeds unmoved
To measure off another Day
For an Approving God.

EMILY DICKINSON

THE LAMB

Little Lamb, who made thee?
Dost thou know who made thee,
Gave thee life, and bade thee feed
By the stream and o'er the mead;
Gave thee clothing of delight,
Softest clothing, woolly, bright;
Gave thee such a tender voice,
Making all the vales rejoice?
   Little Lamb, who made thee?
   Dost thou know who made thee?
Little Lamb, I'll tell thee,
Little Lamb, I'll tell thee;
He is called by thy name,
For He calls Himself a Lamb.
He is meek, and He is mild;
He became a little child.
I a child, and thou a lamb,
We are called by His name.
   Little Lamb, God bless thee!
   Little Lamb, God bless thee.

WILLIAM BLAKE

O sweet spontaneous

O sweet spontaneous
earth how often have
the
doting

   fingers of
prurient philosophers pinched
and
poked

thee
,has the naughty thumb
of science prodded
thy
   beauty   .how
often have religions taken
thee upon their scraggy knees
squeezing and

buffeting thee that thou mightest conceive
gods
   (but
true

to the incomparable
couch of death thy

 173

rhythmic
lover

    thou answerest

them only with

      spring)

e.e. cummings

Spring, the sweet Spring, is the year's pleasant king;
Then blooms each thing, then maids dance in a ring,
Cold doth not sting, the pretty birds do sing,
Cuckoo, jug, jug, pu we, to witta woo.

The palm and may make country houses gay,
Lambs frisk and play, the shepherds pipe all day,
And we hear aye birds tune this merry lay,
Cuckoo, jug, jug, pu we, to witta woo.

The fields breathe sweet, the daisies kiss our feet,
Young lovers meet, old wives a-sunning sit,
In every street these tunes our ears do greet,
Cuckoo, jug, jug, pu we, to witta woo.
    Spring, the sweet spring!

THOMAS NASHE

TO MEADOWS

Ye have been fresh and green,
   Ye have been fill'd with flowers:
And ye the walks have been
   Where maids have spent their hours.

You have beheld, how they
   With wicker arks did come
To kiss, and bear away
   The richer cowslips home.

Y'ave heard them sweetly sing,
   And seen them in a round:
Each virgin, like a Spring,
   With honeysuckles crown'd.

But now, we see, none here,
   Whose silv'ry feet did tread,
And with dishevell'd hair,
   Adorn'd this smoother mead.

Like unthrifts, having spent
   Your stock, and needy grown,
Y'are left here to lament
   Your poor estate, alone.

ROBERT HERRICK

It keeps eternal whispering around
    Desolate shores, and with its mighty swell
    Gluts twice ten thousand caverns, till the spell
Of Hecate leaves them their old shadowy sound.
Often 'tis in such gentle temper found,
    That scarcely will the very smallest shell
    Be moved for days from whence it sometime fell,
When last the winds of heaven were unbound.
Oh ye! who have your eye-balls vexed and tired,
    Feast them upon the wideness of the Sea;
Oh ye! whose ears are dinned with uproar rude,
    Or fed too much with cloying melody,—
Sit ye near some old cavern's mouth, and brood
Until ye start, as if the sea-nymphs quired!

JOHN KEATS

THE GARDEN

How vainly men themselves amaze
To win the palm, the oak, or bays;
And their incessant labours see
Crowned from some single herb or tree,
Whose short and narrow-vergéd shade
Does prudently their toils upbraid;
While all flow'rs and all trees do close
To weave the garlands of repose.

Fair quiet, have I found thee here,
And innocence, thy sister dear!
Mistaken long, I sought you then
In busy companies of men.
Your sacred plants, if here below,
Only among the plants will grow.
Society is all but rude,
To this delicious solitude.

No white nor red was ever seen
So amorous as this lovely green.
Fond lovers, cruel as their flame,
Cut in these trees their mistress' name.
Little, alas, they know or heed
How far these beauties hers exceed!
Fair trees! wheres'e'er your barks I wound,
No name shall but your own be found.

When we have run our passions' heat,
Love hither makes his best retreat.
The gods, that mortal beauty chase,
Still in a tree did end their race.
Apollo hunted Daphne so,
Only that she might laurel grow;
And Pan did after Syrinx speed,
Not as a nymph, but for a reed.

What wond'rous life is this I lead!
Ripe apples drop about my head;
The luscious clusters of the vine
Upon my mouth do crush their wine;
The nectarine and curious peach
Into my hands themselves do reach;
Stumbling on melons as I pass,
Ensnared with flow'rs, I fall on grass.

Meanwhile the mind, from pleasure less,
Withdraws into its happiness;
The mind, that ocean where each kind
Does straight its own resemblance find;
Yet it creates, transcending these,
Far other worlds and other seas;
Annihilating all that's made
To a green thought in a green shade.

Here at the fountain's sliding foot
Or at some fruit-tree's mossy root,
Casting the body's vest aside,
My soul into the boughs does glide;
There like a bird it sits and sings,
Then whets and combs its silver wings;
And, till prepared for longer flight,
Waves in its plumes the various light.

Such was that happy garden-state,
While Man there walked without a mate.
After a place so pure and sweet,
What other help could yet be meet!
But 'twas beyond a mortal's share
To wander solitary there;
Two paradises 'twere in one
To live in Paradise alone.

How well the skilful gardener drew
Of flow'rs and herbs this dial new,
Where from above the milder sun
Does through a fragrant zodiac run;
And as it works th' industrious bee
Computes its time as well as we.
How could such sweet and wholesome hours
Be reckoned but with herbs and flowers!

ANDREW MARVELL

AUTUMN

I saw old Autumn in the misty morn
Stand shadowless like Silence, listening
To silence, for no lonely bird would sing
Into his hollow ear from woods forlorn,
Nor lowly hedge nor solitary thorn;
Shaking his languid locks all dewy bright
With tangled gossamer that fell by night,
    Pearling his coronet of golden corn.

Where are the songs of Summer? With the sun,
Oping the dusky eyelids of the south,
Till shade and silence waken up as one,
And Morning sings with a warm odorous mouth.
Where are the merry birds? Away, away,
On panting wings through the inclement skies,
    Lest owls should prey
    Undazzled at noonday,
And tear with horny beak their lustrous eyes.

Where are the blossoms of Summer? In the west,
Blushing their last to the last sunny hours,
When the mild Eve by sudden Night is prest
Like tearful Proserpine, snatched from her flowers
    To a most gloomy breast.
Where is the pride of Summer—the green prime—
The many, many leaves all twinkling? Three
    On the mossed elm; three on the naked lime

Trembling—and one upon the old oak tree.
Where is the Dryads' immortality?
Gone into mournful cypress and dark yew,
Or wearing the long gloomy Winter through
In the smooth holly's green eternity.

The squirrel gloats on his accomplished hoard,
The ants have brimmed their garners with ripe grain,
And honey bees have stored
The sweets of Summer in their luscious cells;
The swallows all have winged across the main;
And here the Autumn melancholy dwells,
And sighs for tearful spells,
Amongst the sunless shadows of the plain.
Alone, alone,
Upon a mossy stone,
She sits and reckons up the dead and gone
With the last leaves for a love-rosary,
Whilst all the withered world looks drearily,
Like a dim picture of the drownéd past
In the hushed mind's mysterious far away,
Doubtful what ghostly thing will steal the last
Into that distance, grey upon the grey.

O go and sit with her, and be o'ershaded
Under the languid downfall of her hair:
She wears a coronal of flowers faded

Upon her forehead, and a face of care;
There is enough of withered everywhere
To make her bower—and enough of gloom;
There is enough of sadness to invite,
If only for the rose that died—whose doom
Is Beauty's—she that with the living bloom
Of conscious cheeks most beautifies the light;
There is enough of sorrowing, and quite
Enough of bitter fruits the earth doth bear—
Enough of chilly droppings for her bowl;
Enough of fear and shadowy despair,
To frame her cloudy prison for the soul.

THOMAS HOOD

I heard the trailing garments of the Night
    Sweep through her marble halls!
I saw her sable skirts all fringed with light
    From the celestial walls!

I felt her presence, by its spell of might,
    Stoop o'er me from above;
The calm, majestic presence of the Night,
    As of the one I love.

I heard the sounds of sorrow and delight,
    The manifold soft chimes,
That fill the haunted chambers of the Night,
    Like some old poet's rhymes.

From the cool cisterns of the midnight air
    My spirit drank repose;
The fountain of perpetual peace flows there,—
    From those deep cisterns flows.

O holy Night! from thee I learn to bear
    What man has borne before!
Thou layest thy finger on the lips of Care,
    And they complain no more.

Peace! Peace! Orestes-like I breathe this prayer!
  Descend with broad-winged flight,
The welcome, the thrice-prayed for, the most fair,
  The best-belovéd Night!

HENRY WADSWORTH LONGFELLOW

Spirit that breathest through my lattice thou
    That cool'st the twilight of the sultry day!
Gratefully flows thy freshness round my brow;
    Thou hast been out upon the deep at play,
Riding all day the wild blue waves till now,
    Roughening their crests, and scattering high their
        spray,
And swelling the white sail. I welcome thee
To the scorched land, thou wanderer of the sea!

Nor I alone,—a thousand bosoms round
    Inhale thee in the fulness of delight;
And languid forms rise up, and pulses bound
    Livelier, at coming of the wind of night;
And languishing to hear thy welcome sound,
    Lies the vast inland, stretched beyond the sight.
Go forth into the gathering shade; go forth,—
God's blessing breathed upon the fainting earth!

Go, rock the little wood-bird in his nest;
    Curl the still waters, bright with stars; and rouse
The wide old wood from his majestic rest,
    Summoning, from the innumerable boughs,
The strange deep harmonies that haunt his breast.
    Pleasant shall be thy way where meekly bows

The shutting flower, and darkling waters pass,
And where the o'ershadowing branches sweep the grass.

Stoop o'er the place of graves, and softly sway
   The sighing herbage by the gleaming stone
That they who near the churchyard willows stray,
   And listen in the deepening gloom, alone,
May think of gentle souls that passed away,
   Like thy pure breath, into the vast unknown,
Sent forth from heaven among the sons of men,
And gone into the boundless heaven again.

The faint old man shall lean his silver head
   To feel thee; thou shalt kiss the child asleep,
And dry the moistened curls that overspread
   His temples, while his breathing grows more deep;
And they who stand about the sick man's bed
   Shall joy to listen to thy distant sweep,
And softly part his curtains to allow
Thy visit, grateful to his burning brow.

Go,—but the circle of eternal change,
   Which is the life of nature, shall restore,
With sounds and scents from all thy mighty range,
   Thee to thy birthplace of the deep once more.

Sweet odors in the sea air, sweet and strange,
    Shall tell the homesick mariner of the shore;
And, listening to thy murmur, he shall deem
He hears the rustling leaf and running stream.

WILLIAM CULLEN BRYANT

My long two-pointed ladder's sticking through a tree
Toward heaven still,
And there's a barrel that I didn't fill
Beside it, and there may be two or three
Apples I didn't pick upon some bough.
But I am done with apple-picking now.
Essence of winter sleep is on the night,
The scent of apples: I am drowsing off.
I cannot rub the strangeness from my sight
I got from looking through a pane of glass
I skimmed this morning from the drinking trough
And held against the world of hoary grass.
It melted, and I let it fall and break.
But I was well
Upon my way to sleep before it fell,
And I could tell
What form my dreaming was about to take.
Magnified apples appear and disappear,
Stem end and blossom end,
And every fleck of russet showing clear.
My instep arch not only keeps the ache,
It keeps the pressure of a ladder-round.
I feel the ladder sway as the boughs bend.
And I keep hearing from the cellar bin
The rumbling sound
Of load on load of apples coming in.

For I have had too much
Of apple-picking: I am overtired
Of the great harvest I myself desired.
There were ten thousand thousand fruit to touch
Cherish in hand, lift down, and not let fall.
For all
That struck the earth,
No matter if not bruised or spiked with stubble
Went surely to the cider-apple heap
As of no worth.
One can see what will trouble
This sleep of mine, whatever sleep it is.
Were he not gone,
The woodchuck could say whether it's like his
Long sleep, as I describe its coming on,
Or just some human sleep.

ROBERT FROST

Grief

AFTER GREAT PAIN . . . .

After great pain a formal feeling comes—
The nerves sit ceremonious like tombs;
The stiff Heart questions—was it He that bore?
And yesterday—or centuries before?

The feet mechanical
Go round a wooden way
Of ground or air or Ought, regardless grown,
A quartz contentment like a stone.

This is the hour of lead
Remembered if outlived,
As freezing persons recollect the snow—
First chill, then stupor, then the letting go.

EMILY DICKINSON

THE THREE FISHERS

Three fishers went sailing out into the west,—
    Out into the west as the sun went down;
Each thought of the woman who loved him the best,
    And the children stood watching them out of the town;
For men must work, and women must weep;
And there's little to earn, and many to keep,
    Though the harbor bar be moaning.

Three wives sat up in the light-house tower,
    And trimmed the lamps as the sun went down;
And they looked at the squall, and they looked at the
        shower,
    And the rack it came rolling up, ragged and brown;
But men must work, and women must weep,
Though storms be sudden, and waters deep,
    And the harbor bar be moaning.

Three corpses lay out on the shining sands
    In the morning gleam as the tide went down,
And the women are watching and wringing their hands,
    For those who will never come back to the town;
For men must work, and women must weep,—
And the sooner it's over, the sooner to sleep,—
    And good-by to the bar and its moaning.

CHARLES KINGSLEY

MY LAST DUCHESS

FERRARA

That's my last Duchess painted on the wall,
Looking as if she were alive. I call
That piece a wonder, now: Fra Pandolf's hands
Worked busily a day, and there she stands.
Will't please you sit and look at her? I said
"Fra Pandolf" by design, for never read
Strangers like you that pictured countenance,
The depth and passion of its earnest glance,
But to myself they turned (since none puts by
The curtain I have drawn for you, but I)
And seemed as they would ask me, if they durst,
How such a glance came there; so, not the first
Are you to turn and ask thus. Sir, 'twas not
Her husband's presence only, called that spot
Of joy into the Duchess' cheek: perhaps
Fra Pandolf chanced to say, "Her mantle laps
Over my lady's wrist too much," or "Paint
Must never hope to reproduce the faint
Half-flush that dies along her throat:" such stuff
Was courtesy, she thought, and cause enough
For calling up that spot of joy. She had
A heart—how shall I say?—too soon made glad,
Too easily impressed: she liked whate'er
She looked on, and her looks went everywhere.

194

Sir, 'twas all one! My favour at her breast,
The dropping of the daylight in the West,
The bough of cherries some officious fool
Broke in the orchard for her, the white mule
She rode with round the terrace—all and each
Would draw from her alike the approving speech,
Or blush, at least. She thanked men,—good! but
    thanked
Somehow—I know not how—as if she ranked
My gift of a nine-hundred-years-old name
With anybody's gift. Who'd stoop to blame
This sort of trifling? Even had you skill
In speech—(which I have not)—to make your will
Quite clear to such an one, and say, "Just this
Or that in you disgusts me; here you miss,
Or there exceed the mark"—and if she let
Herself be lessoned so, nor plainly set
Her wits to yours, forsooth, and made excuse,
—E'en then would be some stooping; and I choose
Never to stoop. Oh sir, she smiled, no doubt,
Whene'er I passed her; but who passed without
Much the same smile? This grew; I gave commands;
Then all smiles stopped together. There she stands
As if alive. Will't please you rise? We'll meet
The company below, then. I repeat,
The Count your master's known munificence

Is ample warrant that no just pretence
Of mine for dowry will be disallowed;
Though his fair daughter's self, as I avowed
At starting, is my object. Nay, we'll go
Together down, sir. Notice Neptune, though,
Taming a sea-horse, thought a rarity,
Which Claus of Innsbruck cast in bronze for me!

ROBERT BROWNING

MOTHER

Again your kindly, smiling face I see.
Do I but dream? And do my eyes deceive?
Again you whisper through the years to me,
I feel the pressure of your lips at eve.
I dream once more I sit upon your knee,
And hear sweet counsel that I should not grieve;
My hand in yours at twilight time as we
Talk low, and I your sweet caress receive.
At times I see your face with sorrow wrung,
Until, somewhat confused, I scarce believe
That I still dream. Your friends when you were young,
Your own great hopes, your cheer and laughter free
In some weird way are strangely haunting me.
O mother of my childhood's pleasant days!
Still whispering courage and dispelling fears
In daylight hours or quiet moonlight rays,
Are you a dream come from my younger years?
Or do you really walk along the ways,
And know my triumphs, or my inner tears,
That quickly cease when you close by me seem?
Let me sleep on, dear God, if I but dream.

MAX EHRMANN

THE STONE

"And you will cut a stone for him,
To set above his head?
And will you cut a stone for him—
A stone for him?" she said.

Three days before, a splintered rock
Had struck her lover dead—
Had struck him in the quarry dead,
Where, careless of the warning call,
He loitered, while the shot was fired—
A lively stripling, brave and tall,
And sure of all his heart desired . . .
A flash, a shock,
A rumbling fall . . .
And, broken 'neath the broken rock,
A lifeless heap, with face of clay;
And still as any stone he lay,
With eyes that saw the end of all.

I went to break the news to her;
And I could hear my own heart beat
With dread of what my lips might say
But, some poor fool had sped before;
And flinging wide her father's door,
Had blurted out the news to her,
Had struck her lover dead for her,

Had struck the girl's heart dead in her,
Had struck life lifeless at a word,
And dropped it at her feet:
Then hurried on his witless way,
Scarce knowing she had heard.

And when I came, she stood alone,
A woman turned to stone:
And, though no word at all she said,
I knew that all was known.
Because her heart was dead,
She did not sigh nor moan.
His mother wept;
She could not weep.
Her lover slept:
She could not sleep.
Three days, three nights,
She did not stir:
Three days, three nights,
Were one to her,
Who never closed her eyes
From sunset to sunrise,
From dawn to evenfall:
Her tearless, staring eyes,
That seeing naught, saw all.
The fourth night when I came from work,

I found her at my door.
"And will you cut a stone for him?"
She said: and spoke no more:
But followed me, as I went in,
And sank upon a chair;
And curdled the warm blood in me,
Those eyes that cut me to the bone,
And pierced my marrow like cold steel.

And so I rose, and sought a stone;
And cut it, smooth and square:
And, as I worked, she sat and watched,
Beside me, in her chair.
Night after night, by candlelight,
I cut her lover's name:
Night after night, so still and white,
And like a ghost she came;
And sat beside me in her chair;
And watched with eyes aflame.
She eyed each stroke;
And hardly stirred:
She never spoke
A single word:
And not a sound or murmur broke
The quiet, save the mallet-stroke.
With still eyes ever on my hands,
With eyes that seemed to burn my hands,

My wincing, overwearied hands,
She watched, with bloodless lips apart,
And silent, indrawn breath:
And every stroke my chisel cut,
Death cut still deeper in her heart:
The two of us were chiseling,
Together, I and death.

And when at length the job was done,
And I had laid the mallet by,
As if, at last, her peace were won,
She breathed his name; and, with a sigh,
Passed slowly through the open door:
And never crossed my threshold more.

Next night I labored late, alone.
To cut her name upon the stone.

WILFRID WILSON GIBSON

With fingers weary and worn,
    With eyelids heavy and red,
A woman sat in unwomanly rags,
    Plying her needle and thread—
Stitch! stitch! stitch!
    In poverty, hunger, and dirt,
And still with a voice of dolorous pitch
    She sang the "Song of the Shirt!"

"Work—work—work
    Till the brain begins to swim;
Work—work—work
    Till the eyes are heavy and dim!
Seam, and gusset, and band,
    Band, and gusset, and seam,
Till over the buttons I fall asleep,
    And sew them on in a dream!

"O men, with sisters dear!
    O men, with mothers and wives!
It is not linen you're wearing out,
    But human creatures' lives!
Stitch—stitch—stitch!
    In poverty, hunger, and dirt—
Sewing at once, with a double thread,
    A shroud as well as a shirt!

"But why do I talk of Death—
    That phantom of grisly bone?
I hardly fear his terrible shape,
    It seems so like my own,—
It seems so like my own
    Because of the fasts I keep;
O God! that bread should be so dear,
    And flesh and blood so cheap!

"Work! work! work!
    My labor never flags;
And what are its wages? A bed of straw,
    A crust of bread—and rags.
That shattered roof—and this naked floor—
    A table—a broken chair—
And a wall so bland, my shadow I thank
    For sometimes falling there!

"Work—work—work!
    From weary chime to chime!
Work—work—work!
    As prisoners work for crime!
Band, and gusset, and seam,
    Seam, and gusset, and band—
Till the heart is sick and the brain benumbed,
    As well as the weary hand.

"Work—work—work!
  In the dull December light!
And work—work—work!
  When the weather is warm and bright!
While underneath the eaves
  The brooding swallows cling,
As if to show me their sunny backs,
  And twit me with the spring.

"Oh, but for one short hour—
  A respite, however brief!
No blessed leisure for love or hope,
  But only time for grief!
A little weeping would ease my heart;
  But in their briny bed
My tears must stop, for every drop
  Hinders needle and thread!"

With fingers weary and worn,
  With eyelids heavy and red,
A woman sat in unwomanly rags,
  Plying her needle and thread—
Stitch! stitch! stitch!
  In poverty, hunger, and dirt;
And still with a voice of dolorous pitch—
Would that its tone could reach the rich!—
  She sang this "Song of the Shirt."

THOMAS HOOD

GRASS

Pile the bodies high at Austerlitz and Waterloo.
Shovel them under and let me work—
    I am the grass; I cover all.

And pile them high at Gettysburg
And pile them high at Ypres and Verdun.
Shovel them under and let me work.
Two years, ten years, and passengers ask the
    conductor:
  What place is this?
  Where are we now?

  I am the grass.
  Let me work.

CARL SANDBURG

SILENCE

There is a silence where hath been no sound,
There is a silence where no sound may be,
In the cold grave—under the deep, deep sea,
Or in wide desert where no life is found,
Which hath been mute, and still must sleep profound;
No voice is hushed—no life treads silently,
But clouds and cloudy shadows wander free,
That never spoke, over the idle ground:
But in green ruins, in the desolate walls
Of antique palaces, where Man hath been,
Though the dun fox, or wild hyena calls,
And owls, that flit continually between,
Shriek to the echo, and the low winds moan,
There the true Silence is, self-conscious and alone.

THOMAS HOOD

At the mid hour of night, when stars are weeping, I fly
To the lone vale we loved, when life shone warm in
    thine eye;
    And I think oft, if spirits can steal from the regions
      of air
    To revisit past scenes of delight, thou wilt come to
      me there,
And tell me our love is remembered even in the sky.

Then I sing the wild song it once was rapture to hear,
When our voices commingling breathed like one on
    the ear;
    And as Echo far off through the vale my sad orison
      rolls,
    I think, O my love! 'tis thy voice from the
      Kingdom of Souls
Faintly answering still the notes that once were so
    dear.

THOMAS MOORE

GLEE—THE GHOSTS

In life three ghostly friars were we,
And now three friarly ghosts we be.
Around our shadowy table placed,
The spectral bowl before us floats;
With wine that none but ghosts can taste,
We wash our unsubstantial throats.
Three merry ghosts—three merry ghosts—three merry
   ghosts are we:
Let the ocean be Port, and we'll think it good sport
To be laid in that Red Sea.

With songs that jovial spectres chaunt,
Our old refectory still we haunt.
The traveller hears our midnight mirth:
"O list!" he cries, "the haunted choir!
The merriest ghost that walks the earth,
Is sure the ghost of a ghostly friar."
Three merry ghosts—three merry ghosts—three merry
   ghosts are we:
Let the ocean be Port, and we'll think it good sport
To be laid in that Red Sea.

THOMAS LOVE PEACOCK

Farewell, thou child of my right hand, and joy;
  My sin was too much hope of thee, loved boy.
Seven years thou wert lent to me, and I thee pay,
  Exacted by thy fate, on the just day.
Oh, could I lose all father now! For why
  Will man lament the state he should envy?
To have so soon 'scaped world's and flesh's rage,
  And, if no other misery, yet age?
Rest in soft peace, and, asked, say here doth lie
  Ben Jonson his best piece of poetry;
For whose sake, henceforth, all his vows be such,
  As what he loves may never like too much.

BEN JONSON

TO THE MEMORY OF MR. OLDHAM

Farewell, too little and too lately known,
Whom I began to think and call my own;
For sure our souls were near allied, and thine
Cast in the same poetic mold with mine.
One common note on either lyre did strike,
And knaves and fools we both abhorred alike.
To the same goal did both our studies drive:
The last set out the soonest did arrive.
Thus Nissus fell upon the slippery place,
While his young friend performed and won the race.
O early ripe! to thy abundant store
What could advancing age have added more?
It might (what Nature never gives the young)
Have taught the numbers of thy native tongue.
But satire needs not those, and wit will shine
Through the harsh cadence of a rugged line.
A noble error, and but seldom made,
When poets are by too much force betrayed.
Thy gen'rous fruits, though gathered ere their prime,
Still showed a quickness; and maturing time
But mellows what we write to the dull sweets of rhyme.
Once more, hail, and farewell! farewell, thou young
But ah! too short, Marcellus of our tongue!
Thy brows with ivy and with laurels bound;
But fate and gloomy night encompass thee around.

JOHN DRYDEN

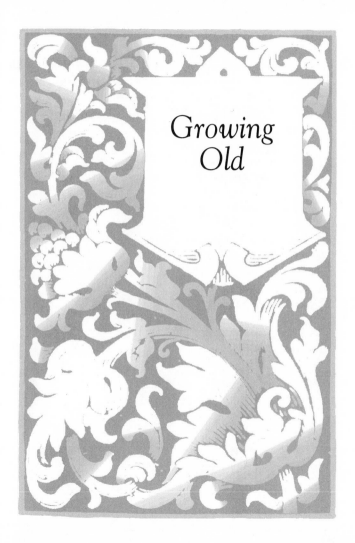

Growing
Old

SONG

When I am dead, my dearest,
    Sing no sad songs for me;
Plant thou no roses at my head,
    Nor shady cypress tree:
Be the green grass above me
    With showers and dewdrops wet;
And if thou wilt, remember,
    And if thou wilt, forget.

I shall not see the shadows,
    I shall not feel the rain;
I shall not hear the nightingale
    Sing on, as if in pain;
And dreaming through the twilight
    That doth not rise nor set,
Haply I may remember,
    And haply may forget.

CHRISTINA GEORGINA ROSSETTI

They are all gone into the world of light!
   And I alone sit ling'ring here;
Their very memory is fair and bright,
     And my sad thoughts doth clear.

It glows and glitters in my cloudy breast,
   Like stars upon some gloomy grove,
Or those faint beams in which this hill is drest
     After the sun's remove.

I see them walking in an air of glory,
   Whose light doth trample on my days:
My days, which are at best but dull and hoary,
     Mere glimmering and decays.

O holy Hope! and high Humility,
   High as the heavens above!
These are your walks, and you have show'd them me,
     To kindle my cold love.

Dear, beauteous Death! the jewel of the Just,
   Shining nowhere, but in the dark;
What mysteries do lie beyond thy dust,
     Could man outlook that mark!

He that hath found some fledg'd bird's nest may know,
    At first sight, if the bird be flown;
But what fair well or grove he sings in now,
      That is to him unknown.

And yet as Angels in some brighter dreams
    Call to the soul, when man doth sleep:
So some strange thoughts transcend our wonted themes,
      And into glory peep.

If a star were confin'd into a tomb,
    Her captive flames must needs burn there;
But when the hand that lock'd her up gives room,
      She'll shine through all the sphere.

O Father of eternal life, and all
    Created glories under Thee!
Resume Thy spirit from this world of thrall
      Into true liberty.

Either disperse these mists, which blot and fill
    My perspective still as they pass:
Or else remove me hence unto that hill,
      Where I shall need no glass.

HENRY VAUGHAN

THE OAK

Live thy Life,
   Young and old,
Like yon oak,
Bright in spring,
   Living gold;
Summer-rich
   Then; and then
Autumn-changed,
Soberer-hued
   Gold again.

All his leaves
   Fallen at length,
Look, he stands,
Trunk and bough,
   Naked strength.

ALFRED, LORD TENNYSON

No Spring, nor Summer Beauty hath such grace
    As I have seen in one Autumnal face.
Young Beauties force our love, and that's a rape,
    This doth but counsel, yet you cannot 'scape.
If 'twere a shame to love, here 'twere no shame,
    Affection here takes Reverence's name.
Were her first years the Golden Age; that's true,
    But now she's gold oft-tried and ever new.
That was her torrid and inflaming time,
    This is her tolerable tropic clime.
Fair eyes, who asks more heat than come from hence,
    He in a fever wishes pestilence.
Call not these wrinkles, graves; if graves they were,
    They were Love's graves, for else he is no where.
Yet lies not Love dead here, but here doth sit
    Vowed to this trench like an anachorite.
And here, till hers, which must be his death, come,
    He doth not dig a grave, but build a tomb.
Here dwells he, though he sojourn everywhere
    In Progress, yet his standing house is here.
Here where still evening is, not noon nor night;
    Where no voluptuousness, yet all delight.
In all her words, unto all hearers fit,
    You may at Revels, you at Council, sit.
This is love's timber, youth his underwood;
    There he as wine in June enrages blood,

Which then comes seasonabliest, when our taste
　　And appetite to other things is past.
Xerxes' strange Lydian love, the Platane tree,
　　Was loved for age, none being so large as she,
Or else because, being young, nature did bless
　　Her youth with age's glory, barrenness.
If we love things long sought, Age is a thing
　　Which we are fifty years in compassing;
If transitory things which soon decay,
　　Age must be loveliest at the latest day.
But name not Winter-faces, whose skin's slack,
　　Lank as an unthrift's purse, but a soul's sack;
Whose eyes seek light within, for all here's shade;
　　Whose mouths are holes rather worn out than made;
Whose every truth to a several place is gone
　　To vex their souls at Resurrection;
Name not these living Death's-heads unto me,
　　For these not ancient but antique be.
I hate extremes, yet I had rather stay
　　With tombs than cradles to wear out a day.
Since such love's natural lation is, may still
　　My love descend, and journey down the hill,
Not panting after growing beauties, so
　　I shall ebb out with them who homeward go.

JOHN DONNE

CROSSING THE BAR

Sunset and evening star,
    And one clear call for me!
And may there be no moaning of the bar,
    When I put out to sea,

But such a tide as moving seems asleep,
    Too full of sound and foam,
When that which drew from out the boundless deep
    Turns again home.

Twilight and evening bell,
    And after that the dark!
And may there be no sadness of farewell,
    When I embark;

For though from out our bourne of Time and Place
    The flood may bear me far,
I hope to see my Pilot face to face
    When I have crost the bar.

ALFRED, LORD TENNYSON

THE END

I sing of ghosts and people under ground,
Or if they live, absented from green sound.
Not that I dote on death or being still;
But what men would is seldom what they will,
And there is farthest meaning in an end
Past the wild power of any word to mend.
The telltale stalk, and silence at the close,
Is most that may be read of man or rose.
Death is our outline, and a stillness seals
Even the living heart that loudest feels.
I am in love with joy, but find it wrapped
In a queer earth, at languages unapt;
With shadows sprinkled over, and no mind
To speak for them and prove they are designed.
I sing of men and shadows, and the light
That none the less shines under them by night.
Then lest I be dog enemy of day,
I add old women talking by the way;
And, not to grow insensible to noise,
Add gossip girls and western-throated boys.

MARK VAN DOREN

Remembrance

REMEMBRANCE

Cold in the earth—and the deep snow piled above thee,
Far, far, removed, cold in the dreary grave!
Have I forgot, my only Love, to love thee,
Severed at last by Time's all-severing wave?

Now, when alone, do my thoughts no longer hover
Over the mountains, on that northern shore,
Resting their wings where heath and fern-leaves cover
That noble heart for ever, ever more?

Cold in the earth, and fifteen wild Decembers
From those brown hills have melted into spring:
Faithful, indeed, is the spirit that remembers
After such years of change and suffering!

Sweet Love of youth, forgive, if I forget thee,
While the world's tide is bearing me along;
Other desires and other hopes beset me,
Hopes which obscure, but cannot do thee wrong!

No later light has lightened up my heaven,
No second morn has ever shone for me;
All my life's bliss from thy dear life was given,
All my life's bliss is in the grave with thee.

But, when the days of golden dreams had perished,
And even Despair was powerless to destroy;
Then did I learn how existence could be cherished,
Strengthened, and fed without the aid of joy.

Then did I check the tears of useless passion—
Weaned my young soul from yearning after thine;
Sternly denied its burning wish to hasten
Down to that tomb already more than mine.

And, even yet, I dare not let it languish,
Dare not indulge in memory's rapturous pain;
Once drinking deep of that divinest anguish,
How could I seek the empty world again?

EMILY BRONTË

WRITTEN IN NORTHAMPTON
COUNTY ASYLUM

I am! yet what I am who cares, or knows?
   My friends forsake me like a memory lost.
I am the self-consumer of my woes;
   They rise and vanish, an oblivious host,
Shadows of life, whose very soul is lost.
And yet I am—I live—though I am toss'd

Into the nothingness of scorn and noise,
   Into the living sea of waking dream,
Where there is neither sense of life, nor joys,
   But the huge shipwreck of my own esteem
And all that's dear. Even those I loved the best
Are strange—nay, they are stranger than the rest.

I long for scenes where man has never trod—
   For scenes where woman never smiled or wept—
There to abide with my Creator, God,
   And sleep as I in childhood sweetly slept,
Full of high thoughts, unborn. So let me lie,—
The grass below; above, the vaulted sky.

JOHN CLARE

They flee from me that sometime did me seek,
    With naked foot stalking in my chamber:
I have seen them gentle, tame, and meek,
    That now are wild, and do not once remember
    That sometime they have put themselves in danger
To take bread at my hand; and now they range,
Busily seeking with a continual change.

Thanked be fortune, it hath been otherwise
    Twenty times better; but once, in special,
In thin array, after a pleasant guise,
    When her loose gown from her shoulders did fall,
    And she me caught in her arms long and small,
Therewith all sweetly did me kiss,
And softly said, *'Dear heart, how like you this?'*

It was no dream; I lay broad waking:
    But all is turned, thorough my gentleness,
Into a strange fashion of forsaking;
    And I have leave to go, of her goodness;
    And she also to use new-fangleness.
But since that I so unkindly am served,
I fain would know what she hath deserved.

SIR THOMAS WYATT

THE SCULPTOR

I took a piece of plastic clay
And idly fashioned it one day,
And as my fingers pressed it, still
It bent and yielded to my will.

I came again, when days were passed,
The bit of clay was hard at last,
The form I gave it, still it bore,
But I could change that form no more.

Then I took a piece of *living* clay
And gently formed it, day by day
And molded with my power and art,
A young child's soft and yielding heart.
I came again when years were gone,
It was a *man* I looked upon.
He still that early impress bore,
And I could change it, nevermore.

AUTHOR UNKNOWN

Dear gentle hands have stroked my hair
    And cooled my brow,
Soft hands that pressed me close
    And seemed to know somehow
Those fleeting moods and erring thoughts
    That cloud my day,
Which quickly melt beneath their suffrage
    And pass away.

No other balm for earthly pain
    Is half so sure,
No sweet caress so filled with love
    Nor half so pure,
No other soul so close akin that understands,
No touch that brings such perfect peace as Mother's
    hands.

W. DAYTON WEDGEFARTH

Lord, Thou hast given me a cell
    Wherein to dwell,
A little house whose humble roof
    Is weatherproof. . . .
Low is my porch as is my fate,
    Both void of state,
And yet the threshold of my door
    Is worn by the poor
Who hither come and freely get
    Good words or meat.
'Tis Thou that crown'st my glittering hearth
    With guileless mirth.
All these and better Thou dost send
    Me to this end,
That I should render for my part
    A thankful heart.

ROBERT HERRICK

THE GOOD GREAT MAN

How seldom, friend, a good great man inherits
   Honor and wealth, with all his worth and pains!
It seems a story from the world of spirits
When any man obtains that which he merits,
   Or any merits that which he obtains.

For shame, my friend! renounce this idle strain!
What wouldst thou have a good great man obtain?
Wealth, title, dignity, a golden chain,
Or heap of corpses which his sword hath slain?
Goodness and greatness are not means, but ends.

Hath he not always treasures, always friends,
The great good man? Three treasures,—love, and light,
   And calm thoughts, equable as infant's breath;
And three fast friends, more sure than day or night,—
   Himself, his Maker, and the angel Death.

SAMUEL TAYLOR COLERIDGE

ELEGY WRITTEN IN A COUNTRY CHURCHYARD

The curfew tolls the knell of parting day,
    The lowing herd winds slowly o'er the lea,
The plowman homeward plods his weary way,
    And leaves the world to darkness and to me.

Now fades the glimmering landscape on the sight,
    And all the air a solemn stillness holds,
Save where the beetle wheels his droning flight,
    And drowsy tinklings lull the distant folds;

Save that from yonder ivy-mantled tow'r
    The moping owl does to the moon complain
Of such, as wand'ring near her secret bow'r,
    Molest her ancient solitary reign.

Beneath those rugged elms, that yew-tree's shade,
    Where leaves the turf in many a mould'ring heap,
Each in his narrow cell for ever laid,
    The rude Forefathers of the hamlet sleep.

The breezy call of incense-breathing Morn,
    The swallow twittering from the straw-built shed,
The cock's shrill clarion, or the echoing horn,
    No more shall rouse them from their lowly bed.

For them no more the blazing hearth shall burn,
    Or busy housewife ply her evening care:
No children run to lisp their sire's return,
    Or climb his knees the envied kiss to share.

Oft did the harvest to their sickle yield,
　　Their furrow oft the stubborn glebe has broke:
How jocund did they drive their team afield!
　　How bow'd the woods beneath their sturdy stroke!

Let not Ambition mock their useful toil,
　　Their homely joys, and destiny obscure;
Nor Grandeur hear with a disdainful smile,
　　The short and simple annals of the poor.

The boast of heraldry, the pomp of pow'r,
　　And all that beauty, all that wealth e'er gave,
Awaits alike th' inevitable hour:
　　The paths of glory lead but to the grave.

Nor you, ye proud, impute to these the fault,
　　If Memory o'er their tomb no trophies raise.
Where through the long-drawn aisle and fretted vault
　　The pealing anthem swells the note of praise.

Can storied urn or animated bust
　　Back to its mansion call the fleeting breath?
Can Honour's voice provoke the silent dust,
　　Or Flatt'ry soothe the dull cold ear of death?

Perhaps in this neglected spot is laid
　　Some heart once pregnant with celestial fire;
Hands that the rod of empire might have sway'd
　　Or waked to ecstasy the living lyre.

But Knowledge to their eyes her ample page
    Rich with the spoils of time did ne'er unroll;
Chill Penury repress'd their noble rage,
    And froze the genial current of the soul.

Full many a gem of purest ray serene,
    The dark unfathom'd caves of ocean bear:
Full many a flower is born to blush unseen,
    And waste its sweetness on the desert air.

Some village Hampden that with dauntless breast
    The little tyrant of his fields withstood;
Some mute inglorious Milton here may rest,
    Some Cromwell guiltless of his country's blood.

Th' applause of list'ning senates to command,
    The threats of pain and ruin to despise,
To scatter plenty o'er a smiling land,
    And read their history in a nation's eyes,

Their lot forbade: nor circumscribed alone
    Their growing virtues, but their crimes confined;
Forbade to wade through slaughter to a throne,
    And shut the gates of mercy on mankind.

The struggling pangs of conscious truth to hide,
    To quench the blushes of ingenuous shame,
Or heap the shrine of Luxury and Pride
    With incense kindled at the Muse's flame.

Far from the madding crowd's ignoble strife,
 Their sober wishes never learn'd to stray;
Along the cool sequester'd vale of life
 They kept the noiseless tenor of their way.

Yet ev'n these bones from insult to protect,
 Some frail memorial still erected nigh,
With uncouth rhymes and shapeless sculpture deck
 Implores the passing tribute of a sigh.

Their name, their years, spelt by th' unletter'd Muse,
 The place of fame and elegy supply:
And many a holy text around she strews,
 That teach the rustic moralist to die.

For who, to dumb Forgetfulness a prey,
 This pleasing anxious being e'er resign'd,
Left the warm precincts of the cheerful day,
 Nor cast one longing lingering look behind?

On some fond breast the parting soul relies,
 Some pious drops the closing eye requires;
E'en from the tomb the voice of Nature cries,
 E'en in our ashes live their wonted fires.

For thee, who, mindful of th' unhonour'd dead,
 Dost in these lines their artless tale relate;
If chance, by lonely contemplation led,
 Some kindred spirit shall inquire thy fate.

Haply some hoary-headed swain may say,
   "Oft have we seen him at the peep of dawn
Brushing with hasty steps the dews away
   To meet the sun upon the upland lawn.

"There at the foot of yonder nodding beech
   That wreathes its old fantastic roots so high,
His listless length at noontide would he stretch,
   And pore upon the brook that babbles by.

"Hard by yon wood, now smiling as in scorn,
   Muttering his wayward fancies he would rove;
Now drooping, woeful-wan, like one forlorn,
   Or crazed with care, or cross'd in hopeless love.

"One morn I miss'd him on the custom'd hill,
   Along the heath, and near his fav'rite tree;
Another came, nor yet beside the rill,
   Nor up the lawn, nor at the wood was he;

"The next, with dirges due in sad array
   Slow through the church-way path we saw him borne,
Approach and read (for thou canst read) the lay
   Graved on the stone beneath yon aged thorn."

THE EPITAPH

Here rests his head upon the lap of earth
  A youth to Fortune and to Fame unknown.
Fair Science frown'd not on his humble birth
  And Melancholy mark'd him for her own.

Large was his bounty, and his soul sincere;
  Heav'n did a recompense as largely send:
He gave to Mis'ry all he had, a tear,
  He gain'd from Heav'n ('twas all he wish'd) a friend.

No farther seek his merits to disclose,
  Or draw his frailties from their dread abode.
(There they alike in trembling hope repose,)
  The bosom of his Father and his God.

THOMAS GRAY

THE GARDEN OF PROSERPINE

Here, where the world is quiet;
    Here, where all trouble seems
Dead winds' and spent waves' riot
    In doubtful dreams of dreams
I watch the green field growing
For reaping folk and sowing,
For harvest-time and mowing,
    A sleepy world of streams.

I am tired of tears and laughter,
    And men that laugh and weep;
Of what may come hereafter
    For men that sow to reap:
I am weary of days and hours,
Blown buds of barren flowers,
Desires and dreams and powers
    And everything but sleep.

Here life has death for neighbor,
    And far from eye or ear
Wan waves and wet winds labor,
    Weak ships and spirits steer;
They drive adrift, and whither
They wot not who make thither;
But no such winds blow hither,
    And no such things grow here.

No growth of moor or coppice,
    No heather-flower or vine,
But bloomless buds of poppies,
    Green grapes of Proserpine,
Pale beds of blowing rushes,
Where no leaf blooms or blushes
Save this whereout she crushes
    For dead men deadly wine.

Pale, without name or number,
    In fruitless fields of corn,
They bow themselves and slumber
    All night till light is born;
And like a soul belated,
In hell and haven unmated,
By cloud and mist abated
    Comes out of darkness morn.

Though one were strong as seven,
    He too with death shall dwell,
Nor wake with wings in heaven,
    Nor weep for pains in hell;
Though one were fair as roses,
His beauty clouds and closes;
And well though love reposes,
    In the end it is not well.

Pale, beyond porch and portal,
    Crowned with calm leaves, she stands
Who gathers all things mortal
    With cold immortal hands;
Her languid lips are sweeter
Than love's who fears to greet her,
To men that mix and meet her
    From many times and lands.

She waits for each and other,
    She waits for all men born;
Forgets the earth her mother,
    The life of fruits and corn;
And spring and seed and swallow
Take wing for her and follow
Where summer song rings hollow
    And flowers are put to scorn.

There go the loves that wither,
    The old loves with wearier wings;
And all dead years draw thither,
    And all disastrous things;
Dead dreams of days forsaken,
Blind buds that snows have shaken,
Wild leaves that winds have taken,
    Red strays of ruined springs.

We are not sure of sorrow;
    And joy was never sure;
To-day will die to-morrow;
    Time stoops to no man's lure,
And love, grown faint and fretful,
With lips but half regretful
Sighs, and with eyes forgetful
    Weeps that no loves endure.

From too much love of living,
    From hope and fear set free,
We thank with brief thanksgiving
    Whatever gods may be
That no life lives for ever;
That dead men rise up never;
That even the weariest river
    Winds somewhere safe to sea.

Then star nor sun shall waken,
    Nor any change of light:
Nor sound of waters shaken,
    Nor any sound or sight:
Nor wintry leaves nor vernal,
Nor days nor things diurnal;
Only the sleep eternal
    In an eternal night.

ALGERNON CHARLES SWINBURNE

DOVER BEACH

The sea is calm to-night.
The tide is full, the moon lies fair
Upon the straits;—on the French coast the light
Gleams and is gone; the cliffs of England stand
Glimmering and vast, out in the tranquil bay.

Come to the window, sweet is the night-air!
Only, from the long line of spray
Where the sea meets the moon-blanch'd land,
Listen! you hear the grating roar
Of pebbles which the waves draw back, and fling,
At their return, up the high strand,
Begin, and cease, and then again begin,
With tremulous cadence slow, and bring
The eternal note of sadness in.

Sophocles long ago
Heard it on the Aegean, and it brought
Into his mind the turbid ebb and flow,
Of human misery; we
Find also in the sound a thought,
Hearing it by this distant northern sea.

The Sea of Faith
Was once, too, at the full, and round earth's shore
Lay like the folds of a bright girdle furl'd.

But now I only hear
Its melancholy, long, withdrawing roar,
Retreating, to the breath
Of the night-wind, down the vast edges drear
And naked shingles of the world.

Ah, love, let us be true
To one another! for the world, which seems
To lie before us like a land of dreams,
So various, so beautiful, so new,
Hath really neither joy, nor love, nor light,
Nor certitude, nor peace, nor help for pain;
And we are here as on a darkling plain
Swept with confused alarms of struggle and flight,
Where ignorant armies clash by night.

MATTHEW ARNOLD

FAREWELL, UNGRATEFUL TRAITOR

Farewell, ungrateful traitor,
    Farewell, my perjured swain;
Let never injured creature
    Believe a man again.
The pleasure of possessing
Surpasses all expressing,
But 'tis too short a blessing,
    And love too long a pain.

'Tis easy to deceive us
    In pity of your pain,
But when we love you leave us
    To rail at you in vain.
Before we have described it,
There is no bliss beside it,
But she that once has tried it,
    Will never love again.
The passion you pretended
    Was only to obtain,
But when the charm is ended
    The charmer you disdain.
Your love by ours we measure
Till we have lost our treasure,
But dying is a pleasure,
    When living is a pain.

JOHN DRYDEN

LONDON

I wander thro' each charter'd street,
Near where the charter'd Thames doth flow,
And mark in every face I meet
Marks of weakness, marks of woe.

In ev'ry cry of every Man,
In ev'ry Infant's cry of fear,
In every voice, in every ban,
The mind-forg'd manacles I hear.

How the Chimney-sweeper's cry
Every black'ning Church appalls;
And the hapless Soldier's sigh
Runs in blood down Palace walls.

But most thro' midnight streets I hear
How the youthful Harlot's curse
Blasts the new born Infant's tear
And blights with plagues the Marriage hearse.

WILLIAM BLAKE

I remember a house where all were good
  To me, God knows, deserving no such thing:
  Comforting smell breathed at very entering,
Fetched fresh, as I suppose, off some sweet wood.
That cordial air made those kind people a hood
  All over, as a bevy of eggs the mothering wing
  Will, or mild nights the new morsels of spring:
Why, it seemed of course; seemed of right it should.

Lovely the woods, waters, meadows, combes, vales,
All the air things wear that build this world of Wales;
  Only the inmate does not correspond:
God, lover of souls, swaying considerate scales,
Complete thy creature dear O where it fails,
  Being mighty a master, being a father and fond.

GERARD MANLEY HOPKINS

MUSIC, WHEN SOFT VOICES DIE

Music, when soft voices die,
Vibrates in the memory;
Odours, when sweet violets sicken,
Live within the sense they quicken.

Rose leaves, when the rose is dead,
Are heaped for the beloved's bed;
And so thy thoughts, when thou art gone,
Love itself shall slumber on.

PERCY BYSSHE SHELLEY

I REMEMBER, I REMEMBER

I remember, I remember,
The house where I was born,
The little window where the sun
Came peeping in at morn;
He never came a wink too soon,
Nor brought too long a day,
But now, I often wish the night
Had borne my breath away!

I remember, I remember,
The roses, red and white,
The violets, and the lily-cups,
Those flowers made of light!
The lilacs where the robin built,
And where my brother set
The laburnum on his birthday,—
The tree is living yet!

I remember, I remember,
Where I was used to swing,
And thought the air must rush as fresh
To swallows on the wing;
My spirit flew in feathers then,
That is so heavy now,
And summer pools could hardly cool
The fever on my brow!

I remember, I remember
The fir trees dark and high;
I used to think their slender tops
Were close against the sky;
It was a childish ignorance,
But now 'tis little joy
To know I'm farther off from Heaven
Than when I was a boy.

THOMAS HOOD

NEUTRAL TONES

We stood by a pond that winter day,
And the sun was white, as though chidden of God,
And a few leaves lay on the starving sod;
　—They had fallen from an ash, and were gray.

Your eyes on me were as eyes that rove
Over tedious riddles of years ago;
And some words played between us to and fro
　On which lost the more by our love.

The smile on your mouth was the deadest thing
Alive enough to have strength to die;
And a grin of bitterness swept thereby
　Like an ominous bird a-wing. . . .

Since then, keen lessons that love deceives,
And wrings with wrong, have shaped to me
Your face, and the God-curst sun, and a tree,
　And a pond edged with grayish leaves.

THOMAS HARDY

THOSE WINTER SUNDAYS

Sundays too my father got up early
and put his clothes on in the blueblack cold,
then with cracked hands that ached
from labor in the weekday weather made
banked fires blaze. No one ever thanked him.

I'd wake and hear the cold splintering, breaking.
When the rooms were warm, he'd call,
and slowly I would rise and dress,
fearing the chronic angers of that house,

Speaking indifferently to him,
who had driven out the cold
and polished my good shoes as well.
What did I know, what did I know
of love's austere and lonely offices?

ROBERT HAYDEN

Pleasant it was, when woods were green,
  And winds were soft and low,
To lie amid some sylvan scene,
Where, the long drooping boughs between,
Shadows dark and sunlight sheen
  Alternate come and go;

Or where the denser grove receives
  No sunlight from above,
But the dark foliage interweaves
In one unbroken roof of leaves,
Underneath whose sloping eaves
  The shadows hardly move.

Beneath some patriarchal tree
  I lay upon the ground;
His hoary arms uplifted he,
And all the broad leaves over me
Clapped their little hands in glee,
  With one continuous sound;—

A slumberous sound, a sound that brings
  The feelings of a dream,
As of innumerable wings,

As, when a bell no longer swings,
Faint the hollow murmur rings
    O'er meadow, lake, and stream.

And dreams of that which cannot die,
    Bright visions, came to me,
As lapped in thought I used to lie,
And gaze into the summer sky,
Where the sailing clouds went by,
    Like ships upon the sea;

Dreams that the soul of youth engage
    Ere Fancy has been quelled;
Old legends of the monkish page,
Traditions of the saint and sage,
Tales that have the rime of age
    And chronicles of eld.

And, loving still these quaint old themes,
    Even in the city's throng
I feel the freshness of the streams
That, crossed by shades and sunny gleams,
Water the green land of dreams,
    The holy land of song.

HENRY WADSWORTH LONGFELLOW

Most sweet it is with unuplifted eyes
To pace the ground, if path there be or none,
While a fair region round the Traveller lies
Which he forbears again to look upon;
Pleased rather with some soft ideal scene,
The work of Fancy, or some happy tone
Of meditation, slipping in between
The beauty coming and the beauty gone.

If Thought and Love desert us, from that day
Let us break off all commerce with the Muse:
With Thought and Love companions of our way,—

Whate'er the senses take or may refuse,—
The Mind's internal heaven shall shed her dews
Of inspiration on the humblest lay.

WILLIAM WORDSWORTH

ENID'S SONG

Turn, Fortune, turn thy wheel and lower the proud;
Turn thy wild wheel through sunshine, storm, and cloud;
Thy wheel and thee we neither love nor hate.

Turn, Fortune, turn thy wheel with smile or frown;
With that wild wheel we go not up or down;
Our hoard is little, but our hearts are great.

Smile and we smile, the lords of many lands;
Frown and we smile, the lords of our own hands;
For man is man and master of his fate.

Turn, turn thy wheel above the staring crowd;
Thy wheel and thou are shadows in the cloud;
Thy wheel and thee we neither love nor hate.

ALFRED, LORD TENNYSON

THE GARDEN OF LOVE

I went to the garden of love,
And saw what I never had seen;
A chapel was built in the midst,
Where I used to play on the green.

And the gate of this chapel was shut,
And "thou shalt not" writ over the door;
So I turned to the garden of love,
That so many sweet flowers bore.

And I saw it was filled with graves,
And tombstones where flowers should be;
And priests in black gowns were walking their rounds,
And binding with briers my joys and desires.

WILLIAM BLAKE

LIFE

I made a posie, while the day ran by:
Here will I smell my remnant out, and tie
      My life within this band.
But time did beckon to the flowers, and they
By noon most cunningly did steal away,
      And withered in my hand.

My hand was next to them, and then my heart;
I took, without more thinking, in good part
      Time's gentle admonition;
Who did so sweetly death's sad taste convey,
Making my minde to smell my fatall day,
      Yet surging the suspicion.

Farewell, dear flowers, sweetly your time ye spent,
Fit, while ye lived, for smell or ornament,
      And after death for cures.
I follow straight without complaints or grief,
Since, if my scent be good, I care not, if
      It be as short as yours.

GEORGE HERBERT

THE NEVERMORE

Look in my face; my name is Might-have-been;
    I am also called No-more, Too-late, Farewell;
    Unto thine ear I hold the dead-sea shell
Cast up thy Life's foam-fretted feet between;
Unto thine eyes the glass where that is seen
    Which had Life's form and Love's, but by my spell
    Is now a shaken shadow intolerable,
Of ultimate things unuttered the frail screen.

Mark me, how still I am! But should there dart
    One moment through my soul the soft surprise
    Of that winged Peace which lulls the breath of
        sighs,—
Then shalt thou see me smile, and turn apart
Thy visage to mine ambush at thy heart
    Sleepless with cold commemorative eyes.

DANTE GABRIEL ROSSETTI